Working with the Angels:

The Young Child and the Spiritual World

THE GATEWAYS SERIES TWO

Compiled from articles published in the Newsletter of the Waldorf Early Childhood Association of North America

The publisher wishes to acknowledge the former
editors of *Gateways* -
Joan Almon, Nicola Tarshis, and Stephen Spitalny.

This book is a collection of essays and articles that
originally appeared in *Gateways* and other publications.
All have been printed with the permission of the authors.

Editor: Susan Howard
Managing Editor: Lydia Roberson
Cover Art: Richard Neal
Cover Design: Dale Hushbeck
Layout and Design: Roland Willwerth
Graphics: Erica Merkling
Text Editing: Barbara Audley, John Minderhout,
Christine Bosch, and Jennifer Kleinbach
Administrative Support: Patti Regan, Melissa Lyons and Anne Jimenez

This publication is made possible through
a grant from the Waldorf Curriculum Fund.

© Copyright Waldorf Early Childhood Association of North America, 2004

Published in the United States by the Waldorf Early Childhood Association of
North America
285 Hungry Hollow Road, Spring Valley, NY 10977

ISBN
978-0-9796232-0-2

10 9 8 7 6 5 4 3 2

All rights reserved. No part of this book may be reproduced in any form without
the written permission of the publisher, except for brief quotations embodied in
critical reviews and articles.

Contents

Preface	*Susan Howard*	v

Working with the Angels

Working with the Angels, Archangels and Archai		3
	Helmut von Kügelgen	
Conversation about Angels and Human Beings		7
	Helmut von Kügelgen	
Finding a Connection to the World of the Angels		15
	Helmut von Kügelgen	
The Meaning of Angels in Education and Self-Education	*Michaela Glöckler, M.D.*	23

The Destiny of the Child in Our Times

Working with the Karma of the Young Child		29
	Margret Meyerkort	
Walking and the Incarnation of Destiny	*Joan Almon*	37
Continuing the Work of the Hierarchies	*Werner Glas*	45
Early Childhood and the Consciousness Soul		49
	Joan Almon	
Threshold Experiences of Children and Adults	*Helmut von Kügelgen*	55
Religion of the Young Child	*Elizabeth Moore–Haas*	59

The Gateway of Birth — the *Sistine Madonna*

Raphael's *Sistine Madonna*: Is It Appropriate in the Kindergarten?	*René Querido*	69
The *Sistine Madonna* in the Waldorf Kindergarten		73
	Joan Almon	
The *Sistine Madonna* - Symbol of the Eternal in Humanity	*Rudolf Steiner*	77

The Gateway of Death —
Working with Death in the Kindergarten

After–Death Care in the Home	*Beth Knox*	81
Helping Children in a Time of Trouble	*Nancy Foster*	83
Helping Our Children and Loved Ones at the Threshold of Death	*Nancy Jewel Poer*	85
A Festival for a Threshold Crossing	*Patricia Owens*	91
Birth Into The Spiritual World	*Nancy Blanning*	95
A Story for Mia,	*Louise de Forest*	97
Grandma's Dream	*Sheila Rubin*	99
For Anastasia and Her Dear Grandmother	*Cynthia Aldinger*	101

The Inner Path

Self-Development as a Basis for the Relationship Between the Child and the Adult	*Michaela Glöckler, M.D.*	105
Through the Eye of the Needle	*Felicitas Vogt*	111
The Path of Inner Schooling	*Jorgen Smit*	121
The Spiritual Foundations of Waldorf Education	*Michaela Glöckler, M.D.*	125

Preface

In 1993, the Waldorf Kindergarten Association of North America published two volumes of articles collected from its Newsletter over a ten-year period from its beginnings in 1983. *An Overview of the Waldorf Kindergarten (Volume One)* and *A Deeper Understanding of the Waldorf Kindergarten (Volume Two)* came to be known affectionately as the "pink" and "blue" books, providing a valuable resource for a generation of practicing and aspiring Waldorf early childhood educators. These two volumes offered study material on the foundations of Waldorf early childhood work and many rich examples shared from the practical life of the kindergartens in North America.

Now a second ten years have passed, and our publishing work is reaching its twenty-first year. Much has developed in our Waldorf early childhood movement. In 1997, the Waldorf Kindergarten Association outgrew its name and became the Waldorf Early Childhood Association of North America (WECAN), in recognition of the ever-widening scope of our activity. This work now extends far beyond the nursery-kindergarten to include birth-to-three programs for parents and children, parent/infant awareness classes, home-based and center-based childcare, pre-natal education, extended care, and work with children in underserved communities and high-risk situations involving homelessness and abuse.

The *Kindergarten Newsletter* has become *Gateways*. Its offerings have included articles on the developing child, working with children, working in community, and the inner development of the early childhood educator. As we review the harvest of these last ten years of *Gateways* contributions, it seems time to gather and share them once again. And thus we are pleased to publish the *Gateways Series*. The series will include articles from past issues, as well as additional contributions that have arisen through conferences and research publications during these past ten years.

We have clustered the contents around themes.

Volume One, *The Young Child in the World Today*, includes articles on the condition of the young child in contemporary society which, despite its apparent advances in the realm of technology, is far less advanced in its understanding of the needs of the developing child. Attention-related disorders, health problems such as asthma and allergies, and increased violence and aggression are evidence of today's threats to healthy child development. Volume One offers perspectives on these challenges from a view of the developing child as a being of body, soul, and spirit.

This is Volume Two - *Working with the Angels: The Young Child and the Spiritual World*. The articles collected here are written by Waldorf educators, doctors, parents and grandparents, and by Rudolf Steiner, the founder of Waldorf education. They explore the thresholds of birth and death, and the relationship of children, parents and caregivers to those who dwell on the other side of the threshold—not-yet-born children, the so-called dead, and the world of the hierarchies, including the guardian angel of the child. We hope that you will find them a source of inspiration in your care for young children, who have so recently arrived from across that threshold, and for supporting families experiencing the death of a loved one.

Volume Three in the *Gateways* Series, *The Developing Child: The First Seven Years of Life,* will be published shortly.

We would like to thank our many colleagues and friends in North America and abroad who have shared their work, first in the Newsletter and now in the *Gateways* Series.

It is our hope that the *Gateways* Series will provide inspiration and support to those who carry the profound and wondrous responsibility of caring for the youngest among us, wherever that work takes place in our human community.

Susan Howard, Editor

Working with the Angels

Working with the Angels, the Archangels and the Archai

Helmut von Kügelgen

In the first three years of life, before the child is so engrossed in material life, it has a close relationship with the angels. At night, while asleep, the children meet their angels. They dream of them or have other experiences of them. As we grow up, the qualities of our childhood mature and develop in us and can evolve as imagination, inspiration and intuition. We too can relate to the angels. It generally happens in our sleep, for it is such a remarkable experience that we might be filled with fear if these contacts were to happen in our waking life. Hence, in the Bible, when Gabriel visits Mary, he begins by saying, "Fear not."

In our waking state, we can work in such a way that our relationships to the spiritual world is strengthened, both to the angels and to the human souls who have died and are living in the world of the spirit. This relationship can manifest in our daily life in various ways. For example, in the German language, when one receives a sudden idea one says it has *eingefallen*—"fallen in." But what has fallen in and from where has it fallen? This can be the work of the angels, pouring their thoughts into mankind, or it can be the help of those human souls who are now in the spiritual world but wish to help us and work with us.

The spiritual world is always there around us, and we can work more consciously if we note the transition as we move from the earthly world to the spiritual world and vice versa. Thus at night we can say as we enter sleep, "Now I am entering the spiritual world," and in the morning as we awaken, we can say, "Now I am entering the earthly world."

We can also connect with the angelic world during the moment before we walk into our classroom. There can be a moment of absolute silence before entering into our work. Our hearts can quicken, and we can say a prayer. For a moment one can think of the angels, or of a friend who is now in the spiritual world. Then one goes with a renewed strength into one's work.

In working with the spiritual world, it is important to work in a rhythm, and particularly the rhythms of seven are a great help. One can work with the rhythm of seven days or seven years or even seven minutes. Seven months, however, would not be a true rhythm. We are not yet so far along that we can observe ourselves over a period of seven lifetimes and work with that rhythm. In rhythms of seven a new strength appears. We can work with meditations in seven-day rhythms, such as with the Foundation

Stone meditation. Rudolf Steiner gave the Foundation Stone meditation as a whole, but then showed how one can work with it in seven day rhythms. In this way one connects with it more fully. If one is trying to work with a number of verses or meditations, such as the *Foundation Stone,* the *Calendar of the Soul,* and the *Verse for the Dead,* one can put them into rhythms of seven. Thus, the Verse for the Dead could be said each Saturday, rather than each day.

When we work with these rhythms of seven, the angels take notice of us. If, for example, we have a sudden impulse to act, we can take time and wait seven minutes before acting. We may then feel that seven minutes is a very long time indeed. But in this quiet pause something happens. Waiting these seven minutes gives the angels a chance to notice us, to let something "fall into" us. In this way we make time for the angels to enter into our lives, and they wait for us to do this. It is not that magnificent revelations from the angels appear to us in this time, but that the angels *see us*. They can only perceive us when we are prepared for this to happen and give it time.

In 1919, Rudolf Steiner said that our century is particularly important during the age of the consciousness soul. It is a time when our consciousness can open up to the realms of nature and to the higher hierarchies. All of this can happen in quite a new way, now that the angels no longer take an interest in the form of man as they did in the past. We must consciously work on ourselves so that the angels can take an interest in us again.

We need to realize that every child, every colleague, every parent is more than just a physical being. Every one contains a spiritual being as well, which brings something with it from previous earth lives. Recognizing the spiritual nature of other human beings is a prerequisite for finding our connection to the spiritual hierarchies.

Rudolf Steiner went on to say we should not overload ourselves with the rational thoughts of the intellectual soul era, which is now past. We need to open up to the thoughts of the consciousness soul, recognizing the living spirit in each of us and recognizing our connection with the hierarchies of the spiritual world. When these thoughts are taken up by us with inner strength, they can help us in our work with the parents and help us lead the children rightly into their new lives on earth. In this context we must realize that it is not our task to educate according to state regulations, nor are we a "program," or simply a method. In the highest sense we work in accordance with the angels, the archangels and the archai. It is these beings of the third hierarchy who employ us, who give us our work. They work with us as individuals, and they work with us as a faculty. Their presence is acknowledged in the *Teachers' Imagination,* which is used by the College of Teachers in a Waldorf school.

As Waldorf educators we work with these beings of the third hierarchy: the angels, the archangels and the archai, but all humanity has a new opportunity to work with them. Since the fifteenth century, we have been in the age of the consciousness soul. This age will last over two thousand years, but Rudolf Steiner indicated that the twentieth century was an especially important time for humanity to lift up its awareness to the spiritual and begin again to work consciously with the beings of the heavenly world. One way to do this is to include the angels in our planning for the next day. In the evening we can not only review what has happened during that day, we can preview what is to come next. We can also have a conversation with our angel. Rudolf Steiner said the angel would then grow interested in what is coming. It does not matter if in the morning we forget what was said during the night, for the angel will not have forgotten it. When we need the insight given, it returns to us at the right moment. The angel leaves us free, but works to help us, for example, to really understand one another when we are in conversation. Later, our thoughts may be filled with loving forces that awoke in this conversation. This too is the work of the angel.

A good preparation for this inner work is to practice control of thinking. Rudolf Steiner describes this exercise in several of his books. Self control in the realm of thinking helps us to receive insights from the angels. We may then suddenly experience that the angelic beings give us the courage to do something which we would not otherwise have had the strength to do. As teachers it is a help if we study the biographies of individuals. In know-ing the life of another, one begins to see how the angels worked into a human being's destiny, often in remarkable ways.

When we study the destinies of a nation or a people we can see the working of the archangels, for they guide the work of whole groups. They guide the development of language, where the spirit of a people is reflected. They also guide the development of language in each individual. Thus it is important to pay attention to speech, so that it is true and beautiful. Our speech can be a fine work of art. Archetypal creativity lies in the word. Rudolf Steiner was always very careful about how he spoke, even in his everyday exchanges. It is especially important how we speak with young children, for they are finding their way into language. We speak to them in whole sentences, and in the good, fine way of fairy tale language. Speech itself can give courage, for it connects us with the archangels, the spirits of time.

We can work with the beings of the third hierarchy in many ways. As Waldorf teachers we work with the *Teachers' Imagination*, which refers to the angels, the archangels, and the archai. As individuals we can make space for a relationship with the third hierarchy. At night, for a few seconds before sleep, we can think: "The angels, archangels and archai *want* to help me in my daily work." In the morning we can think of these beings again and remind ourselves that they want to help us if only we are open to receiving their help. In this way we find the courage for our work.

Dr. Helmut von Kügelgen spoke on the human being's relationship to the hierarchies at a conference in Dornach at Easter, 1991. The lecture referred to in this article is entitled "The Waking of the Human Soul and the Forming of Destiny," and was given by Rudolf Steiner in Prague on April 28, 1923. Dr. von Kügelgen spent thirty years as a teacher at the original Waldorf school in Stuttgart, and was the founder of the International Association of Waldorf Kindergartens. He also served as Director of the Waldorf Kindergarten Seminar in Stuttgart and edited a collection of booklets on the festivals and the inner life of Waldorf teachers, now available in English as the Little Series. *This translated article was reprinted with permission from the International Waldorf Kindergarten Association.*

A Conversation about Angels and Human Beings

Helmut von Kügelgen

Cornelia Handler: *In our time we are so oriented intellectually and materialistically, yet angels seem to be making their comeback again. To speak about angels today is no longer taboo. Although there is a danger of showing them in a kitschy, mawkish or even demonically distorted way, their true appearance touches us very deeply, especially in art. Has there not always been something mysterious about angels?*

Helmut von Kügelgen: I think that the greatness and power of spiritual experiences touches the limits of human beings. What is experienced as suffering and destiny is one reality. The other reality is that time in human history has progressed. It is a fact that we originate from the spiritual world, from the heavenly world, from the world of spiritual beings—whichever way we might wish to describe it. Yet we seek our incarnation and our destiny here on earth. I think this becomes particularly apparent at the two gates: the gate of birth and the gate of death.

At the gate of death there is something gazing in from the spiritual world that can be called angels, or the world of beings, or of spirit. There are also beings at the other gate, the gate of birth. During my childhood it would have been impossible to talk so openly about birth and abortion, about being born or not being born, as is now done in the newspapers. On the one side come voices that say, "My womb belongs to me!" On the other side, the language from Rome and the Pope does not fit into our time anymore.

In modern destinies, where these kinds of questions thrust themselves into life, the experience of the spiritual world becomes so strong that it craves for a tangible form. A way emerges. There is a remembrance of the heavenly world as something orderly and containing the fullness of spiritual and of divine powers. It is a fact that the border of consciousness with the spiritual world is somewhat sore or chafed. Embracing the spiritual world is a part of human existence—trying to live with the awareness that there is something in the spiritual that belongs to the human being.

As human beings we are also open towards the earth. Through evolution, we carry stones, plants, and animals in us. Our physical nature includes the material nature, the stillness of the mineral realm, which we can see and touch. Furthermore, we have in us all the secrets of growth, development, death, and continuous change, in which we can summarize the secret of the plant world. Also, we have a kind of life in us that we share with the animal kingdom, sensitive to feelings and passions. For humanity to realize that all physical life on earth developed during the course of evolution has been a tremendous discovery. Now it is important to see how the spiritual individuality is incarnating into this life. It is this individuality that we call the I. If you observe this accurately, you will get a trace of the angels. I do not mean exactly what appears in art and literature. What appears in art and in poems—of Rilke, for example—can give us overwhelming impressions.

Handler: In our conversation, I would like to seek the entrance to the world of angels mainly in the immediate, human, living experience. Do you know of angel experiences that refer to the time of expecting the arrival of a child?

Von Kügelgen: Here you can clearly notice the difference between humans who live with the reality of a spiritual world, and those who always close their mind to it. Of those who are simply open, you always hear that they know certain things. They may say, for example, "I conceived on this particular night." Women are generally more open to spirituality than men, and especially in this area, because they are the ones who conceive. They often know exactly when the human being is beginning its journey. Sometimes they hear the name of the child. It is amazing how this happens. Often you have to keep on seeking for the name and finally it is given through a godfather. Another time you are absolutely sure. Much depends on whether human beings open up to experience something. It is hard for spiritual beings—if I may say it this way—to penetrate closed doors. What little children sometimes tell or what you experience yourself, does not enter into consciousness. There are far more spiritual experiences than you may suspect.

Handler: What relationship does this little child have to the world of angels before self-awareness awakens?

Von Kügelgen: If you look at the little child, there is still a very simple way to see what happens. The child arrives in a little body that heredity provides. This body is then further formed by the individuality from the spiritual world, even into the fingerprints that serve to distinguish individuals. Then the little child experiences three large steps in becoming a human being, which continue to repeat in life in certain ways; it learns to walk, to talk, and to think. The first requires a tremendous will power for life and activity. Nobody taught the child all the secrets that establish a connection with the will. The question is whether you can explain everything as a reflection of the physical, or if you can experience it from the spiritual realm. If you watch closely, you can see that movement always emerges from the spirit and not from the material. Then you realize that something has been brought along from the time before birth. If you think of the living divine, you can say that the incentive for the will was given before the conception of this spiritual individuality. The power of the self is the will: the will that unites, the will to love, and the will to live. And then it is strange to observe that children who have been born around a certain time form a generation all over the world. Sometimes you see this very clearly, as in the youth movements around the world in 1968, movements that changed the world. This will of the individual has something to do with the spirit of time.

Every human being, whether a materialist, a Bolshevik, a nationalist, or an idealist, can talk about the spirit of time. But it is of utmost importance to understand very clearly that the spirit always emerges from an individual. Spirit is individual. The divine spirit or the heavenly hosts, as they are called in the Christmas story, are present at the growing of a seed as well as at the birth of a human being. The powerful creator of beginnings (in Greek: Archai), the great spirit of time, is the initiating spirit. It is this being that bestows the will. Because of it the organs move, the first breath is taken. Activity begins, a will activity that nobody taught to the child, and that the child brought along somehow. This will has to be taken up through the working of the environment by educators and parents until the child is around two–years–old—the defiant age. The will must be handled in such a way that it can then be implanted in the self.

Provided they have not been damaged, we can perceive the second deed as language emerges from children with an elemental force. The movement of the body leads to the movement of speech, which develops in the interplay between the child and its environment. Even there, we are used to speaking of the folk spirit, of the speech spirit. Usually you say that communities have a spirit (e.g., a class spirit, a school spirit) that animates and inspires the group. This super–personal being has been called an archangel. And then it is astounding, over and over again, how fast children pass over to thinking. This is the third deed, which is actually very personal: the relation of our thinking to our individuality, our unique genius. Here is the sphere where all the other things are taken into consciousness, where we form our world view, where we are led more and more to freedom by our guardian angel.

Thus the spirit of time watches over our decisions and activities, the spirit of community over our feelings and speech, and the spirit of personality over our thinking. Let me just use the names of the old tradition: the custodians of the three fountains of our daily life—will, speech, thinking—are the archai, archangels, and angels, respectively. These are beings of the third hierarchy, the part of the spiritual world closest to human beings.

Handler: How do we stay in contact with our angels?

Von Kügelgen: Well, you stay in contact with them by being found by them while sleeping. The world of angels leaves the human being more and more free as he or she grows up, because the human being is called to freedom. Freedom is most difficult, and the angels do not always intervene. Therefore it is easier to speak of guardian angels in relation to children. They continue to accompany you. The older you get, however, the more you are left to take your own will, your feeling, speaking and your thinking under your own responsibility, into your own hands. For this purpose you need the help of these spiritual beings whom you usually do not encounter while you are awake, but while you are asleep. And you only find them if you have gone to sleep worthily, if you have experienced some idealism in your thinking—something spiritual—and if your feelings and your speech have been touched by the center of your heart. If you have performed such good activities you encounter these angel realms in sleep.

Handler: One can gain rich experience with children at kindergarten age. Could you tell us something from your personal experience?

Von Kügelgen: I want to tell what a mother wrote to me some time ago about her four-year-old child and his brother of six months. The older one came creeping into the mother's bed one morning and said, "Last night I dreamed of an angel that was so beautiful." "Oh," said his mother, "You dreamt about your angel?" "No," replied the child, "I cannot see him, since he holds me in his arms. No, about your angel." That left the mother speechless, and she did not know what to answer. She paused for a moment. Then the child said: "You know, mother, we are all the same size over there, you and I and Frieder." The mother was simply shocked. She is a mother who doesn't speak much about angels. But she lives with the reality of the spiritual world, and that enables her child to talk about such dreams. I have experienced something similar, even in the first and second grades and in religion lessons. If you really listen inwardly to what the children say, then the most incredible experiences come to light. This requires you to be open and not silence children, as happens frequently when they tell such things. If they notice that the adult does not want to hear anything about it, they remain silent.

Handler: Can we, as "well-informed parents," prevent children from having such experiences?

Von Kügelgen: That's right. An attitude that denies the divine, spiritual world, or only accepts as reality what you can feel through the physical senses, lets the openness for other beings die. Children are completely open, and in this state they perceive our thoughts as well. We have to learn again to experience the reality of thoughts. In former times people used to pray for others or they cursed them. Everybody knew that when other people are thinking of me, they assist me, they support me. Thoughts are elemental beings. They are, so to say, those natural beings, who also have had names in the old tradition: sylphs, elves, and so on. And so thoughts are spiritual beings who come and go. Every thought has a reality. And when the reality of the spiritual world surrounds the children, it has incredible value for the inner world of the child. For the child notices not only the outward activity, but also thoughts and feelings.

Handler: Before we talk about the duties this entails for the adult, I would like to take a look at the development of the child. How does the relation of the child to the spiritual world change during the child's development? Could you relate a little more from your personal experiences?

Von Kügelgen: Yes, the best way is to use this or that example for it. I am thinking of a boy, an "early bird," who was awakened too early. These are children in whom you can experience certain things as examples. This boy was incredibly awake and well-informed in his childhood. His father was a physicist, and you had the feeling that very early the child was deeply familiar with technical things. He possessed a precocious, even perfected way of speaking. You could think, now, this is a completely awake and well-informed child who knows all the tricks of adults. Then he reached the third grade and made himself a doll in handwork lessons. He developed a personal relationship to the doll, as you only see in little children. The doll had to go to sleep with him. He talked to it. There opened to him a world of angels, the possibility to encounter dwarves, all kinds of questions concerning St. Nicholas, the infant Jesus, and so on; all these are living and inwardly moving realities in the feeling and fantasy life of the child. You can experience with this example that children do not have to lose the spiritual world. The child always experiences the living being in everything: in every plant, in every stone, in every little stick. A spiritual world is spread around the child. Today—and here is something for adults to address—when we speak about St. Nicholas or the infant Jesus, we often do this for the purpose of fooling the child. "For surely," we may think, "there is no world of angels, but I am talking to the child about it, as if it were true."

With children you can still celebrate Christmas, because then you can talk about the infant Jesus and related things. When children become well-informed this passes. Nowadays it often happens this way. You can talk about it, however, in a way that you feel the power and the love to complete the dollhouse or the play kitchen at midnight from the one who is love. The infant Jesus is not just "something," but the magic of the forces of love that I actually draw from in this world. Then there is a transition for the child, and the realization that father and mother made the things does not come as a shock, but as something very natural. I experienced this with my own children. My oldest daughter said later on, "I knew everything already, you know, but I didn't want to know it. My little brothers and sisters should have it as beautifully as I had it!" You have to know that love is actually alive among us in the representative of humanity, the Christ. If I absorb this and then start talking about the infant Jesus, then it is just something very real. This acceptance of the spiritual world as real is what I called openness before. Under this condition these beings of the spiritual world can really take part.

Handler: Yes, how you describe this is beautiful. You notice that the child does not suddenly have the experience, "What I learned from my parents is not true." The child's point of view changes, and spiritual things still can exist when parents have the right relation to them.

Von Kügelgen: I think this is the point. As an adult I have to acquire the truth of the divine, spiritual world, the truth of God's messengers, the world of angels. Today this is not granted freely any more. Tradition has become so dull and empty, ending up with Santa Clauses in every department store. These are ghosts; this is terrible! We have to conquer the truth of the spiritual world. And there is the question how we are able to grasp the truth behind the image. God the Father is not an old man with a beard who sits on a golden throne after all. We have to re-conquer this. We have to get away from the compulsion to materialize images in order to reach real experiences again. When the great poets had experiences of angels, they felt tremors shaking the foundations of their being. If you are really allowed to look into the divine world of beings, you understand that the first thing these beings tell you in the Christmas story is always, "Do not be afraid! For lo, I come from a land of angels to proclaim something to you." These angels are not cute, they are not baroque cherubs. When they become visible they stir and shake us most deeply in the depths of being.

This world, where children come from, is still very close to them. I think I can experience how close the world of angels is to children. When children imitate, they direct all their will power to see how we behave. They live in this will, "I just have to be and act like my surroundings, then everything is well." This habit is carried over from the spiritual world, where the children found themselves in the good hands of spiritual beings. Now it echoes in their ability to imitate. When you observe this you are sad at not being an angel yourself. You feel you should try to be an example for the child. But it is not easy to guide the life of children in the way the angels have done. You have to be conscious that responsibility is transferred slowly from the hands of the angels. You guide the children to independence through education for some years, and then release them into maturity.

How many things were given to you somehow impulsively in the form of changes and conversions when you were young? This slowly ends in the twenties. Then you have to work on these gifts. You have the feeling the angels still watch you and intervene in your fate from time to time. You get a push. But actually the point is to form a conscious contact with the spiritual authority that guides your destiny. It is not so important that we have experiences of angels, but that the angels experience us. This is important. You can hardly endure these angel experiences. But it is important to be open, so they can help you.

Handler: Can you tell us about a concrete event where the help of an angel appears?

Von Kügelgen: I will tell you an example given by Rudolf Steiner. It was during the time of the foundation of Waldorf education. Rudolf Steiner was in Berlin. There were many questions concerning the foundation of the Waldorf School. Then Steiner said, "The relationship we have to our own genius, to our own angel, is different from that of earlier millennia, of earlier cultures. Since the arrival of the modern age—about the middle of the fifteenth century, when natural science and technology as we know them began—the relationship to angels changed." Steiner thought that everybody, not just teachers, ought to know this.

In fact, angels are more interested in what we do the next day than in what occupies us in our review of the past day. You should ask, "What can I do better tomorrow?" We prepare the next day with our angels during the night. Maybe we have an appointment the next day at noon, a very important conversation. In sleep you consult your angel and prepare something together. Then you wake up next morning having forgotten everything, of course. One might ask, "How do you save what must not be forgotten?" Rudolf Steiner's answer was, "It does not matter if you forget it. The angel is the one who did not forget." Then, when you get into the important conversation, you have confidence because the angel lets something "fall" into you. You have an idea, and the right word comes at the right moment. What is more beautiful and more important than to have the right idea at the right moment? The German language has a marvelous expression for this kind of sudden idea: "Einfall" (literally, something falling in). Here you can ask, "Who let it fall in?" This was the angel.

The relationship to the spiritual world is an acquired one. It has to do with the religious in general, which has a will-filled nature. Religiousness is either of will nature, which means it leads to action, or it is not religious. The will, the action, always moves towards the future. That is the interesting aspect of angels; they want to link you to the future.

Handler: *The student looks into the future as soon as school releases her. She becomes independent and forms her own destiny. Questions are no longer answered by the teacher. Pain and suffering are part of the adversities in his life. Trials and strokes of fate often place humans before seemingly unanswerable questions of life. Can you say something about this?*

Von Kügelgen: I think the most important thing in dealing with your own fate is to notice that strokes of fate, pain, and suffering have to do with your own individuality. When pain and suffering occurs we have to tell ourselves over and over again, "This matters to me, this is a call for me. I shall learn something from it." If we do not have this relation to the angels, who always accompany our fate, then, when pain and suffering hit, we only look around and ask, "Who is guilty?" Then the guilt is always laid on somebody else. We believe we can accomplish something by exposing somebody else, or even taking revenge, instead of saying, "Somebody else might be guilty, but this deed holds meaning for me. I have to accept it." If you look back in life, you often find that, although not easy to accept in the moment, the importance of the event becomes evident later. If you look back you might experience something similar to the young man who lived on the fat of the land from the money of his father. Then the father became bankrupt, and the son suddenly had to care for himself. At first he was angry and cursed. But later, when he was forty-four years old, he said, "For heaven's sake, had that not happened, what would have become of me! I would have drowned in the drug scene, or something else, if my father had not become bankrupt." What he cursed earlier, he blessed when he looked back on his life.

In such a moment, when you can bless

pain and suffering, it is as if behind the events you can feel the face of the angel and the flapping of wings. Then you may be able to help the one who caused the problem, by forgiving. You walk straight up to the person and forge links between you despite what has happened. Then you realize how much salvation can result from this, because in this moment you accept the smaller, outer pain and the greater, deep suffering. These are also "Einfalle," things falling in from the realm of angels.

Often one speaks of the guardian angel and thinks, "When disaster comes, the angel will arrive and protect me." This is correct with little children, who do not have a conscious relation with the heavenly world. They have an angelic relation, or a direct relationship, which pertains to the unconscious will. Yet children are sometimes led into suffering; they are not always protected. We should not see all this pain and suffering as caused by enemies. Pain and suffering and ultimately death approach us from the spiritual world as helpers, as friends. Of course, one could say, "You are sitting in comfort on a dry and beautiful chair right now. It is warm and it is easy to say something like this in such a moment." But you have to think about it calmly. When you have a look at your life in moments of composure, then such thoughts can become substance at your disposal. When pain and suffering fall upon you, then you can remember this. Be strong now, and also accept the help of the angel who asks no more of you than you can bear. This is forming the right relationship.

Handler: This is the way the adult consciousness can deal with pain. Explain how it is with the child and about pleasure and joy.

Von Kügelgen: Pleasure and joy are important for us as adults—for children they are essential. But we must not make the mistake that we are entitled to pleasure and joy the same way we are to pain and suffering. We should think of them as gifts of "the gods," as grace. "Oh, what a blessedness to be loved and to love, gods, what a blessedness!" This exclamation of Goethe should flare up in thankfulness from the hearts of children. Thankfulness is the seed of all good habits. Thanks also to the help of angels when you learn to accept and affirm pain and suffering. Children still reach consciously for this help. It is important for us to cultivate serenity before sending the children into sleep, with a verse, a prayer, or a song, If you do this with all seriousness, then the child can have real spiritual experiences, like the child who said, "No, I can't see my angel, for he holds me in his arms." Sometimes it is sad to hear parents say they do not pray with their child. They just want to let the child decide on his own whether he wants to pray or not. During the time when this bridge has to be built, something is missing.

It is different in adolescence, a time when the young person has to build up distance and try out the most absurd things. The adolescent asks himself if something is still reaching in from childhood like a deep, inner being. This area, which we earlier called the guardian angel, this spiritual world that we heard about in legends, tales, mythologies, the gospels, and so on, now begins to appear as one's own deeper force.

Handler: You also spoke about the helping forces in relation to death. Could we, in conclusion, have a look at the Angel of Death?

Von Kügelgen: As I told you, Rudolf Steiner spoke about the fact that in our times something has changed in relation to the spiritual world and the world of angels. Angels do not force themselves upon us when we become mature, rather they wait for us. You have to acquire a relationship to the spiritual world. This is not simply given to you as a gift. In this way of acquisition the dead are of great help, however. Conrad Ferdinand Meyer captures this in his poem, "Choir of the Dead," where he shows that the dead continue to be interested in what happens on earth, in the people with whom they lived together. Love can build bridges, for love has just this spiritual character. Here we can cultivate the relation to the dead. It is something really wonderful when you can accompany people over the threshold of death. It is incredible, that just as there has been a first breath at birth, there is now the last breath at death, and suddenly the body is abandoned. Sometimes a last seal of individuality forms at death so that you just realize in this moment who has been living with you. The great difficulty is that we really do not have a proper sentiment for the moment of death. The same way a new generation appears on earth through birth, so the further fate starts with the moment of death. Not to be able to die for years, to wait for the right moment, in all these mysteries lies the knowledge of angels whether a fate has been accomplished. The angel of death is the angel of eternal life, of spiritual individuality. Therefore, you see, there are so many questions about the intensive care unit and about everything that relates to death, also about these widespread deaths in wars that continue to rage around us.

This way, you have to say, the attempt to come to terms with it really requires a deep knowledge of fate. And we only gain this form from the relationship with angels. We have to acquire this, it will not be given to us as a gift. It is wonderful when you are shown so much through the spiritual science of Rudolf Steiner, from the research of this man. This helps you to open up to your own experiences and your own quest, and to research the question of fate.

To summarize: The finding of the right relationship to the angels hinges upon how we will bring something to them. Only in this way can they form something in our life. Through such a relationship they have the opportunity to play a part and we want to grant them this.

Dr. von Kügelgen spent thirty years as a teacher at the original Waldorf school in Stuttgart, and was the founder of the International Association of Waldorf Kindergartens. This translated article was reprinted with permission from the International Waldorf Kindergarten Association.

Finding a Connection to the World of the Angels

Dr. Helmut von Kügelgen

We hear of the many changes that have taken place in Waldorf education. The winds of change are also blowing in Eastern Europe.[1] It is called *Perestroika,* the restructuring. George F. Kennan has spoken of Perestroika and its founder, Gorbachev, in this way: "This is an age of change and Gorbachev has made him-self its angel and its instrument." Gorbachev has brought the greatest changes imaginable in Russia and in Eastern Europe, but what is meant here by "angel?" And what is the spirit of this time?

Rudolf Steiner had twenty-three people before him when he started the lectures known as the *Study of Man.*[2] These are a preparation for the educational work of this age, for this epoch. His opening personal remarks have only recently been included in the English translation of the lectures. He said that now, at the very beginning of this preparatory work, it behooves us to come into contact with the spiritual powers through whose power and at whose mandate each of us must work. We must ask them to stand behind us as we seek to work out of imagination, inspiration and intuition.

What does it mean to find contact with the spiritual powers? Rudolf Steiner spoke of these powers, of the angels, the archangels, and the third hierarchy. True, we have these words, we know their names. But George Kennan has the words, too, but he probably does not actually believe in angels. In the New Testament, the angel appears to the shepherds. In doing so he opens the door to a new level of consciousness. The angel says, "Do not fear," for it is a shock to behold an angel and to have this door opened, but it is a good shock. The intent is not to destroy but to open the soul and heart (imagination), and to enable one to hear (inspiration). Now the will of the spiritual world can work in our will (intuition). We know that accidents can come into our lives and shock us in this way. A scientist has recently written that if we take a frog from its pond and put it in a pan of hot water it will jump out. But if we put it in a pan of cold water and heat it slowly, the frog will sit there in the water until it has boiled to death. The frog's senses are such that it can distinguish large temperature changes but not gradual ones. There has been no need in its evolution to distinguish small temperature changes. Today, the scientist continued, the human race is like the frog in the pan. Human beings are not really paying attention to the fact that we are gradually destroying life on the planet. We are destroying the living world in the Amazon region, for example, but we are not noticing what we are doing.

Likewise, we live in the world of the spiritual hierarchies, but we are not aware of them. They live in us, but we are not sensitive enough to perceive them. How can we contact the spiritual powers who are with us in normal life? Rudolf Steiner has said we have to contact them if we are to take up this new task of educating for our times. How can we perceive the connection? We can look back, reflect, and see that there is guidance in our life. Where there is guidance, there is a guide. We then get the first feeling of a guardian angel in our life. It does not just come of itself. We must do something to discover it.

With children it is easy to speak of a guardian angel. They still live at another level of consciousness where they can experience the hierarchies. Recently, I received a letter from a former kindergarten teacher who is now a mother of three young children. The oldest was four or five, the second child was three, and the baby, Frieder, was eight months old. One morning the eldest child came into the mother's bed and said that during the night he had seen a most wonderful angel. "Oh, you've seen your angel," said the mother. "No, not my angel. I was in the arms of my angel. It was your angel I saw." The child was silent, then paused and said, "There we are all of the same height, you and I and little Frieder." The mother dared not answer. Children have such experiences, but often they cannot find those with ears to listen. This mother could listen.

When the adult is striving to find spiritual contact, this forms a bridge for children. It helps them to preserve their own contact with the spiritual world. The light of God the Father comes through the angel to the child. This nearest hierarchy is a bridge that allows us to go deeper and deeper into higher worlds.

Both adults and children have other close ties with beings in the spiritual world, that is with those who have recently died. It may be a grandparent or a friend. This is not always sad, and we must not look melancholic when we speak of death. Death can be celebrated. We can speak of the grandmother having gone home, from where she can now look down upon us. There is a feeling of love when we remember the deceased, and this gives us the imagination of the beloved person. We feel we are in the spiritual world, or at least that it is near to us and not far away. It is the home we never lose. Feelings of reverence and awe are important when we speak of a person who is dead, so that the children can live with these feelings as a reality.

The other feeling that is most important in building a bridge to the angels in the spiritual world is thankfulness. Rudolf Steiner did not say that we must teach the children to say thank you, but rather that, as adults, we must learn to feel grateful for life. We must feel thankful to live in this world, to have this work, to have our destiny, even the difficult parts. Life brings pain and things not easy to endure. But when we love our task of educating children, our work will be full of thanksgiving. It is necessary that out of this gratitude we come to love truth and be as true as we can be. This is one of the most important things for the teacher. Real truth is in the spiritual world, and the striving towards truth is a striving towards the spiritual world.

Another way to help children to keep their connection with the spiritual world is to bring them rightly into the world of sleep at night. We adults also draw near to the archangels at night, but it is the content of our speech that brings us into connection with them. Little children cannot do this by themselves. The verse or prayer that we say with them or for them at night helps lead the child to the archangels.

As adults we can review the day before

going to sleep. As we look back over the day, or even over longer periods, we begin to discover the guidance in our lives. Every day we can consider, "What did I do? Could I feel a guiding force?"

Rudolf Steiner has said that in modern times, since the beginning of the age of the consciousness soul in the fifteenth century, it is not only necessary to look back with our angel but to look forward—to prepare the next stage. For example, if we have an appointment the following day with the parent concerning their child, then we look ahead to this appointment with our angel the night before. We do not then think, "What did my angel tell me? What ideas did my angel give me?" It is not for this that we think ahead with our angel, but to carry this mood into our meeting, the mood of living together with our angel at night. We must still struggle and think on our own, but if we live in this mood, we will find the right way. We can bring through the night and into the day a mood that says, "The angels are always with us." With this picture before us then, suddenly the frog is aware that there is heat and must jump. In this mood we can become more attuned to small, incremental changes. It is as if the frog becomes aware of the rising temperature and jumps. When we recognize the spiritual reality in our thoughts, we can bring this spiritual reality into our deeds.

The greatest mysteries of how we interact with the angels, the archangels, and the archai, arise with respect to how we walk, talk, and think. When we walk we use muscles—we move, we incarnate into the carne, the flesh. Our karma enters into our body. The child experiences this in the first year of life as he or she begins to move and to walk.

To speak is to engage in a finer movement. This is the beginning of the whole life of art. How are the words produced—out of love or out of anger? In speaking, spiritual content or concepts are in our words. The beings and concepts of the spiritual world do not come out of our heads—the world that surrounds us is spiritual as well as material.

When we think we open ourselves to the spiritual world. For the child, thinking is first bound to the things in the immediate surroundings. With maturity thinking changes, as does the sequence of thinking, feeling and doing. As adults we normally think first, then feel and then act. Sometimes we are like children and act first. Then we think: "What have I done?"

We are faced with the tasks of this generation, for we must be contemporary. We are part of this time period. In this way, as we perform deeds, we have contact with the spirit of our time, the archai. When we speak, we have contact with the spirit of the people of a community, with the archangels who work with communities of people. When we think, we come into contact with our own angel. We also come into community with the whole of mankind. We bring thoughts into the whole of language. Thus, through thought we make contact with our angel. Through speech we make contact with the archangels. Through activity we make contact with the archai, the spirits of our time.

Rudolf Steiner once described the task of anthroposophy as bringing together communities that they may work to become a chalice for the higher beings of the spiritual world. In Switzerland, when the first Waldorf School was three years old, Rudolf Steiner said that people didn't understand what was meant by the free spiritual life. Everyone thinks it means each rooster stands on his own dung heap and calls cock-a-doodle-do. That is not free spiritual life. In a school, there are teachers who work together through the college of teachers or faculty. Perhaps one teacher has a more pronounced part, another a less pronounced part. But they are working together for the spirit of the school. They work together to bring this spirit to work through the deeds of the everyday life of the school.

To understand a school, a gathering of teachers, we should consider the picture of Pentecost, the gathering of souls connected to the Christ and his Resurrection. This was a community fulfilled in a higher being. That is the task of anthroposophists.

In the beginning of this talk, man was likened to the frog, not a very nice image. But we need to see that we are surrounded by the spiritual world, not just at the moment when the angel speaks and opens the door, but in all the gradual ways in which we experience the spiritual world. When we think, when we feel, when we act, then we are experiencing the spiritual world and its beings. In all that we call self-education, we experience sensitive steps toward the beings of the third hierarchy.

In his lecture *Awakening to Community* (given on December 13, 1923), Rudolf Steiner describes the path of anthroposophy. For the adult it begins with thinking. Then art is called forward to enliven the thoughts and concepts. It ends with a religious deepening, with warmth that reassures the heart. Thus it begins with what the head can grasp, takes on all the life and color of the artistic experience, and ends in warmth that suffuses and reassures the heart so that man can feel that the spirit is his true home. Rudolf Steiner said, "The present world rejects this approach and, as a result, anthroposophy has its enemies."

Now we arrive again at the beginning of this talk and the *Study of Man*. Rudolf Steiner spoke of the need for connecting with spiritual powers, on whose behalf and at whose mandate each of us works. He gave the *Teachers' Imagination,* the meditation that connects the college of teachers with the angels, the archangels, and the archai.

Rudolf Steiner told the teachers not to forget how we work together with the hierarchies: with our own angel behind us, with the archangels forming a chalice of courage, and with the archai bringing a drop of light into that chalice. In this way we too can work individually with the third hierarchy. Every evening before doing our own meditation we can think: "The angels, archangels and archai will help me to do the work I must do." In the morning, after our meditation, we can think again, "The beings of the third hierarchy will help me." In this way we come into connection with angels, archangels and archai. That is the answer that Rudolf Steiner gave to the theme of this conference.

When did Rudolf Steiner give the *Teachers' Imagination?* What is its background? In 1919 Rudolf Steiner gave the *Study of Man* course. He gave thanks to the spirits who gave Emil Molt the idea of founding the first Waldorf School. (Molt was the director of the Waldorf Astoria cigarette factory and asked Rudolf Steiner to speak there about the threefold social order. When the workers became interested in Steiner's ideas about education, Molt helped finance a school for the children of the workers.) In his last words, Herbert Hahn, one of the original Waldorf teachers who had already given lectures to the factory workers repeated: "Don't forget that Waldorf education comes from the threefold social movement." Out of this movement Emil Molt had the idea to have a Waldorf school. Already in 1907, in *The Education of the Child,* Rudolf Steiner planted the seeds for such an education by claiming, when called upon to do so that spiritual science would be able to give a complete grade school curriculum. He waited to be asked, and Molt asked him.

Is the Archangel Michael a spirit of time? Yes. He has been an archangel and he is now ascending to the realm of the archai, the spirits of time. His old name was Archangel Michael. Now it is better to speak of Michael, for he is no longer an archangel.

How do spiritual beings guide us? They whisper inwardly. We need to have a receptive inner mood and to be prepared to hear them. Then we have ideas and inspirations. We see a child playing in a corner. Suddenly he bounds up and goes elsewhere. Where did his new idea come from? We experience this when we sit and think about a child with a difficulty. How can we help him? An idea comes. Ideas are not simply the perspiration of our brain, something our brain excretes. Thoughts are in the world and we have the mental ability to be aware of them. There are many concepts, such as what is beautiful and what is ugly. We learn by looking at the world, by seeing what lies behind and within the things of the world. We need to cultivate fantasy in the young child, for it sheds light on all.

How do we know who is guiding us? Might it be a harmful being? How can we recognize it? Yes, there are evil beings who try to guide mankind. On the one side we have Ahriman, the cold force of hardening. On the other side we have Lucifer, full of fire and light, intoxicating and ecstatic. It is like the cross of Golgotha between the other two crosses. We must learn to make the distinctions between them, for there exists the possibility of error and temptation. We have the burden of freedom and we must learn to distinguish.

Does our nightly meditation as teachers help bring the children into the arms of their angels? Yes, and even if you think of persons who have died, you are helping to build the connection to the spiritual world. We can ask that our love be united with the love of Christ; or we may help a person who has died to give aid in bringing a child, in sleep, into the arms of its angel. On the next day the children may come to you in another mood, as if you had been together in the night.

Are there children who cannot find their angels? Rudolf Steiner has said that children are in the arms of their angels until they begin to think in a materialistic way. When children are young, the angel is more active in finding them. As we grow older, the angel recedes in order to leave us free. If we do not try to make contact, the angel withdraws more and more. This is the dark side of "freedom."

What is the spirit of the community? In the *Teacher's Imagination* we speak of the circle of the archangels forming a chalice. This is a verse worked with by colleges of teachers, and in a college the members come out of different communities; they have different languages or come from different social communities, yet they are striving to work with the spirit of the school. We can speak
of the spirit of a class, or of a school, or of a conference, and this spirit comes about as we work together. Then we arouse the interest of the hierarchies and they say, "There is good work. Let us go and help there."

How much can we say to children about spiritual beings? This is a question of tact. We can speak out of our inner conviction and tell, for example, a birthday story. But it must be real. We must know about the spiritual world and the angels who dwell there. We mustn't talk about it because we're "supposed to."

In relationship to the last question, what about our speaking of elemental beings? They too are real and we must find our relationship to them. Our thoughts are also little beings which live in the natural processes. This is a very large question, however, and cannot be dealt with adequately now. Bronja Zahlingen spoke of finding Marjorie Spock's book, *Fairy Worlds and Workers,* very useful for those wishing to understand the elemental beings more fully.

You spoke of looking forward in a meditative sense. How do I do this? One aspect of this question is very practical. We get up in the morning, eat our breakfast, enter our kindergarten, and prepare for the day. We can also think ahead for the next day by communicating in the evening with the hierarchies and again in the morning. Then it is possible for our angel to add new ideas, so that we can do the right thing in the moment, or if necessary, do something other than we had prepared.

What if one is working alone and does not have colleagues or a college of teachers? You are part of the whole kindergarten movement, so you are not alone in this work. It is important that we all feel we are working together for the pedagogy of the future. Then we can experience the chalice referred to in the *Teachers' Imagination.*

Why do we suffer so often from physical illnesses in our striving upward? Consider the plant. As it grows up toward the light its upper leaves are the thinnest and most delicate while its lower leaves, nearest the earth, are the largest and most solid. Likewise, as we grow upward toward the sun and the spirit, our physical body may grow weaker. It is important to have the right relationship with the spirit and with our own karma.

Gratitude is an important quality in this relationship to joy and delight. We have to develop gratitude because we never merit joy and delight; they are always the grace of the gods. But when pain and suffering come, we will know that this belongs to our karma; we merit it. Pain and suffering will help us to progress. We must not flow away into the spiritual world in a luciferic way. We must find the middle way, standing on the earth while striving upward and with thankfulness for the grace of joy and delight.

What about thinking about children before we go to sleep? Freya Jaffke spoke to this question and said each person must find their own way with this. The picturing of the children should not take too long, though one can then spend more time on a difficult child. For example, one can review a problematic moment with the child, make it "present" within one, picturing the "gesture" of the moment. How did the moment arise? What led up to it? What happened during the moment and what came afterwards? Also find a good moment that happened with the child. Make this picture "big" before your mind's eye. Thus two objective pictures stand before you without any wishes. Then you can feel a real connection to the child. You may do this picturing several nights in a row. Maybe one picture will increase or decrease; or both may merge into equal strength. Then daily work will grow easier, for you are not fighting the one aspect. But be careful not to neglect the "good" children. Look at all of the children, and occasionally dwell on one or two who do not have difficulties.

> Remember daily that you are continuing the work of the spiritual world with the children. You are the preparers of the path for these young souls who wish to form their lives in these difficult times. The spiritual world will always stand by you in this task. This is the wellspring of strength which you so need.
>
> *Rudolf Steiner*
> *(Discussions with Teachers)*

1. This lecture was given in 1989, before the end of Communism and the vast changes in Eastern Europe.

2. These are now included in a new edition of the lectures entitled, *The Foundations of Human Experience,* Anthroposophic Press, (Hudson, NY, 1996), pp. 45-48.

Dr. von Kügelgen spent thirty years as a teacher at the original Waldorf school in Stuttgart, and was the founder of the International Association of Waldorf Kindergartens. This translated article was reprinted with permission from the International Waldorf Kindergarten Association.

The Meaning of Angels in Education and Self-Education

Dr. Michaela Glöckler

When we picture angels we see them wearing light garments and having graceful movements. They are light-filled beings with wings. In pictures by the old masters angels are usually seen walking on the earth, not floating above it as the other hierarchies do. Angels are not lazy. They do things, things generally interpreted as being joyful, such as singing. This is a clue for us, for we come closest to the angels when we experience joy. Rudolf Steiner said we must envisage light, a white garment, and a light-filled countenance, graceful movements and wings. If we do this every day and immediately let the picture go again it will then begin to tell us something.

How do angels affect our teaching in Waldorf education? We should look at what the child does and says, because this is the message the angels send us. Our inward response should be, "What do you want me to do for you today?" In the morning one has certain plans for the day ahead, but these do not always happen. At night we try to make a picture of what really happened during the day. Look at it and see what it tells you of yourself.

It is important to learn from this that you cannot ask yourself to be what you are not. Self-education is only fruitful if you work within your abilities and recognize who you are. Be honest with yourself—no more and no less. When we look at the children, we do not want them to be different. We accept them for who they are. We must be equally honest with ourselves and not strive for impossible ideals. Naturally, one needs a goal to direct for one's steps, but the goal must not be unattainable. Never think that you have arrived at your goal. If this is your belief, then other people will not like you and social life becomes impossible. It is important to see reality as little steps but with spaces of freedom in between.

How does the angel come near to us to bring us the message? The process of uprightness is the message. This can speak to us through an inner imaginative activity. Humans are an egg shape standing on its narrow end. We are top heavy, but we do not fall over. Through our senses we hold our balance. Nature does not hold us upright, as can be proved when we lose our balance through lack of sleep or use of drugs. We are the ones who have to hold ourselves upright. We are predisposed towards this freedom, and that gives us the upright ability.

We experience feelings of sadness, anger, and happiness, but we need to work on them to create a balance, not swing from one to the other. The sensation of feeling in itself is nothing. It is in what we do with feeling that our freedom manifests itself.

We have thoughts on many subjects such as war, stars, mechanics, et cetera. If we are asked whether we have seen an angel, we would probably answer "No," yet we have thoughts and that is where the angel lives—in our thoughts, memories, conscious biography, impulses, or ideals, for example. Our thoughts and our thinking are the being of the angel. Angels are totally selfless. They go with us where we go and leave us in freedom. They just accompany us.

There is a relationship between angels and water. At the pool of Bethesda it is said that an angel moves the water once a year. The angels are often connected with water, and water is a picture of selflessness. Seventy percent of the human body is water. It is everywhere in creation and makes life possible. At death, water leaves the corpse, goes back into the clouds, comes back as rain and goes where it is needed. Our selflessness should also be like that, and we should go where we are needed.

We perceive nature through our senses. Many people think that after death it will be the same, but we need to be ready for a different form of perception. On Earth, we can only begin to perceive how the angels see us. On earth we are nourished by plants and animals; we take the world inside us. The nourishment of the angels is different; it is what they get from us. They need this for their work. Our soul life is there for the angels; they watch our feelings and our deeds. Perhaps sometimes you feel you do not want to be watched all the time, or feel you want to help them but cannot. You might want to say, "Don't look today—look tomorrow when I can do it better!" We must try to see our own life with the eyes of angels, but the angels will never interfere, for we have the freedom to act as we feel right. The angels develop through truth and freedom. Selflessly they look at the little things we do manage to accomplish.

The angel works in our astral body and, in turn, gives us something to work with. The colors are given to us, but we have to paint the picture ourselves. If we did not have ideals we would look at people as animals or machines. The ideal of brotherhood or sisterhood means that we become more human. Without ideals we do not act in a human way. We also need the confidence that other human beings have an external resistance and are developing.

We should approach our nightly review of the day's happenings as we would examine a landscape. It should be without sympathy or antipathy. The aim is to be objective, not to do it with happiness or anger. "Shake hands" with your angel and hope that tomorrow will be better, for each night we prepare the following day with our angel.

Many people think that the past was wonderful, or at least spiritually better than the present. The difference between past and present lies in the way we think. In the past, people saw the spiritual beings and lived with them consciously. Nowadays, our thought is blind to the spiritual world. We have to find new ways to see the angels and we have to want to find them again. For this we need to engage our will. If we can find this, it will give us back our inner orientation and have an effect on our bodily life here. At night, when we meet, our angel tells us to watch out during the day and to find freely what was given in the night. We must be alert for this during the day. Rudolf Steiner said we get all the strength we need for the coming day at night if we don't destroy it ourselves.

Do not find the negative. Find good in

everything and then you will find the angel. If you do this it is like a quiet conversation.

How does this relate to the festival of Whitsun (Pentecost)? This is the festival fifty days after Easter, when the apostles were together and the spirit came to them. They were then able to help others. It is thinking that came to the apostles. Thought is an independent language and breaks the barrier of other languages. This is related to the second coming of the Christ, which is often portrayed as taking place in the clouds. Clouds are water and air and serve as a picture of the etheric world. The ego has to work with the thoughts, but they live in the etheric. The second coming of Christ will take place in any case, but the question is how we can consciously perceive it. If we think of ideals and morals (i.e., spiritual thoughts), then we meet the etheric Christ.

The angels live with us in thinking these moral and ideal thoughts. In old legends the Christ appears and helps. You can be sitting at home concerned and worried, and a new thought comes that gives you courage. Then you have met encountered your angel bringing the message from Christ.

An important aspect of education is to awaken thinking. Thinking gives us an orientation for the spiritual world. In the past the priests and wise men did it, but now we need to do it ourselves. We have to give the child this confidence and ideals and know that the angels will give us strength for our life—especially for work with the children. The strength comes in the night. We have to have confidence in our thinking during the day. The message of the angel is the message of our thinking.

Dr. Michaela Glöckler is currently the head of the Medical Section at the Goetheanum, Dornach, Switzerland. She has been active as a pediatrician and school doctor in Germany and is the author of A Guide to Child Health, *Floris Books*

*The Destiny of
the Child in Our
Times*

Working with the Karma of the Young Child

Margret Meyerkort

Emotions obscure the spirit
And withdraw forces from the physical body.
The soul needs peace.
The spirit needs to be uplifted in gratitude
The body needs the calmness
Of trust in Karma forces.

Rudolf Steiner, 1924

It was Rudolf Steiner's intention to awaken contemporary people to a Western and modern view of karma. Therefore it is my intention, indeed my hope—in spite of the mood of questioning—to further our own interest in the mystery of karma, or much more, the majesty of karma. I propose four steps:

1. To remind ourselves of what karma is;
2. To look at the karma of becoming an earthly human being;
3. To look at the karma of being modern;
4. To look at personal karma.

Karma is the realization of prenatal resolutions made in the presence and with the help of creator beings. These resolutions shape outer appearance, movements, the language one speaks, the people one meets, one's profession, race, nationality, et cetera.

Here is a story from life. Jack had a student friend, Ann. Jack knew Ann's older sister Jill. She lived by herself and preferred the company of people in their forties. Jack had seen her once or twice at a student gathering. Then came a New Year's Eve Party, and Jack asked Jill if she would go with him. She was undecided because she had agreed to go out with Peter. Then Peter rang and was lukewarm about going out at all that evening. "OK, Peter, don't bother to fetch me," said Jill and went out with Jack. The party was boring and together, with some friends, they went to another party at a large apartment. At one point Jack passed through a dark corridor where Jill was lying on a sofa. He sat down by her. Later on they kissed. After an hour he took Jill to her bus and he walked home. He wondered what this experienced woman had felt, what was in store for him the next time they met. But she realized that her life had taken a decisive turn and she would never like to be without him. A few years later they married, and Jill became a dependent partner, one who was reluctant to stand on her own two feet.

What do such stories show us? Jack and Jill took steps independently of each other and with entirely different motivations. A number of other people were involved in the final outcome. Peter was not keen to go out.

The first party was boring. The second party provided the darkened room. Jill felt tired. None of the participants had the slightest idea that they helped to shape the future of two people. Jack and Jill could say that karma works gently, and yet sometimes there is an unbelievable push. Karma weaves without the participants' discernment. It is imperceptibly active and we have to cope in such a situation. I repeat—this is the reality of karma—suddenly I am in an unforeseen situation and now I have to cope. After our birth, we are formed and transformed from two sides. Karmic forces work out of the cosmos into our uniquely individual incarnation, while, equally, we are formed by the empathetic effects that parents and teachers have on us and by the empathetic effects of our physical surroundings.

Here is another story: After the Second World War a young Hungarian woman escaped to the West. She married and had a little boy. Three years later the young mother died of cancer. The father was desperate with grief. "Why? How can I go on? What for?" John was four years old when father and son traveled by car through the country. "Look, Daddy, what's that?" "That's a pine tree." "There's another pine tree." "No, that's a beech tree." "Why, Daddy?" "The wind has different names. In one country the wind is called Maria, in another Mistral. And so the trees have different names—oak tree, beech tree, pine tree." Silence. And then John said, "And John and Daddy and all people have one name." "And what is that?" "Jesus." What spoke through the child? Was it a cosmic force, common in all human beings, to live, grow, and develop? Or did the child, through the empathetic interweaving with his physical surroundings, react in this way to the father's sorrow?

My second point is that we all go through a karmic process of a human incarnation where cosmic and earthly forces interweave. We are sensitive to our physical body. We appreciate its beauty and sensitivity, its strength and versatility. But many of us also agree that in our age we experience an assault on this instrument of our physical existence.

In his book, *An Outline of Occult Science*, Rudolf Steiner describes how, during the incarnation of the Earth called "Old Saturn," the basis of the physical body of the human being was laid down. It was shaped in such a way that it could be the vehicle for perceiving the Earth and for bearing the ego. Later, in a lecture given in 1908, Steiner calls the structural system of bones, muscles and nerves, and the physiological system of breath, blood, glands, and metabolism, "The Name of Man."

Let us look at the "Name of Man" from the point of view of the structural system. What was it that was laid into it? Functions like the lifting of the head, the lifting of the trunk, crawling, the upright position, walking. At first it is a struggle to gain physical equilibrium, to acquire a free and freed orientation. Gradually the human being learns to control his movements and attain a balanced position between heaven and earth. This struggle for the upright position in space is at the same time the beginning of an endeavor that lasts a lifetime.

It is of help to consider first the peculiar relationship in the human being of legs and feet to arms and hands. The legs and feet continue to serve the movement of the body in space, while arms and hands are liberated from this function, which allows them to serve the inner life of the human being. They afford the possibility for the soul to find its equilibrium. Thus, we may say: "What was laid into the upright position of the human being was freedom."

This is the karmic potential with which we are born. In other words, what is common to all mankind is that, each time we breathe in "The Signature of the Gods," we listen to "The Name of Man" as it has been laid into our structure. The karmic potential is to develop and to sound forth anew "The Name of Man"—the bearer of freedom.

To the teachers of the first Waldorf School, Steiner said, "It is your task to continue the work of the creator beings." With regard to our present consideration this means that it is the task of the human community to see to it that the structural system can be a faithful image of the plan, of the love, and of the work of the divinities. Then the personal karma of the human being can enter this physical organization.

Now, each time the human being incarnates she does so into a time situation of her particular environment, into a specific age. She finds then and there a given situation. What is this today? Today we have trampolines and skating boards for young children and bouncers for babies. Do these gadgets allow the young child to find equilibrium in space or do they disturb the postural system and thereby interfere with the karma of the child?

A child can develop a steady walk if she has the opportunity to walk through mud, across brooks and pebbles, through snow, and across ice. We must offer our little ones opportunities to refine bodily movements by climbing, falling, jumping over puddles, and crouching under fences. Do we offer opportunities to refine arm movements, hand movements and finger movements in sweeping and shoe polishing, in sewing and tying a bow? These and many more fine motor skill movements build the physical body for a balanced position in space, and in turn build the foundation for the development of language. (See *Challenge of the Will*, Margaret Meyerkort and R. Lissau)

Let us take a brief look at the development of language. Again, the creator beings have laid a seed into the human being, the possibility to communicate through language, the possibility to speak. We share in this karma. More than that, for the actual acquisition of language we all need the community of human speakers. This means that if language is really to come about on Earth, each of us requires a social component. In this need of the child and this response of the adult, human beings the world over share. How does this look in our modern age? Do we encounter attacks in this realm, too? What happens when babies are laid on their tummies and there is no communication between child and adult? What kind of language does the child hear by way of technical devices? Is it blunted? Is it dead? Surely, it is absolutely and totally impersonal. How can we realize the potential of language, how can we continue this "Signature of Creator Beings?" There are many ways. One is that we teachers must step up our work with the parents.

Here is another story. Recently a therapist working with a school said to a parent and teacher: "Tom should never have been admitted into this kindergarten because of his speech difficulties." Maybe! But another consideration would have been, creator beings interweave gently with our karma, and, inasmuch as we are co-workers of creator beings, does it not behoove us to develop a sensitive (and respectful) manner of working? Can we not step up our work so that it helps us to recognize both—karma as a fact and also the manner of karmic activity? In other words, it is one thing to tell a parent that statistics have shown that many or most of today's speech difficulties are no longer hereditary but due to parents no longer speaking to their offspring. But it is an entirely different thing to interact with a particular parent and to empathize with a particular child as I try and remove their obstacles. If I make the needs of the parent and child my own, the potential for communicating through language gently unfolds.

I have already touched upon one feature of my third point, but "the karma of being modern" is much greater. As a soul incarnates into an age she tries to unite herself with the meaning of that age, its spirit, so that she may live "out of" the forces of that particular Time Spirit. Thereby she may grow, serve, and develop her fellow human beings and the Earth. "To be modern" poses then the following question: How can a soul within the ongoing stream of time intuit the intentions of creator beings, and how can she, within the ongoing stream of time, give shape and form to the intentions of creator beings? The question addresses both the spiritual and physical worlds.

Steiner shows us that in 1879 mankind entered a new age, which proceeds under the guidance of the creator being Michael. As students of Steiner we may ask, why might a soul choose to incarnate into this century in the western world? What might a soul wish to develop, indeed need to develop in this Michaelic Age?

One faculty that each of us can acquire under the guidance of Michael is self-reliance. It is to grow into an autonomous personality, a person who can take responsibility for his own actions. Our forefathers were dependent on what the church said, on the laws set by the chieftain, on the code of behavior prescribed by the family or nation. People lived without any questions in their communities; they lived—as it were—with answers. In those times, the human being lived unquestioningly within the blood community: "Uphold the name of the family, continue the profession of the father or be an outcast."

To some extent this was still so with the adults in Steiner's time, because they had incarnated before 1879, i.e., into a Gabrielic Age. This meant that these people largely lived by rules of behavior, and this in turn meant that they gave their own children an authoritarian education. I remember the stories my own parents, born in 1898 and 1903, i.e., into a Michaelic Age, stories of enormous tensions in the home between themselves, as children of a Michaelic Age, and their parents, souls of a Gabrielic Age. Through these tensions a strengthening of the soul forces occurred. Of course, the opposite could also occur, a crushing of the personality, and often it did occur.

Today the little ones in the kindergarten are the third or fourth generation to be born in the Age of Michael. Their parents and their grandparents already incarnated with this longing to grow self-reliant. Is this why, since the middle of this century, adults have become increasingly anti-authoritarian in their approach to child rearing? What is clear to me is that an anti-authoritarian society has sapped the children's strength. How is that possible? Ours is a permissive society—"Take what you want out of the refrigerator," or, in answer to Sally's "I'm not going to bed": "OK, then." We adults constantly cave in when the child whimpers, "I want ballet lessons," or "I'm not going to paint." This disallows the child to meet the realities of existence; it disallows the child to relate to his surroundings. Instead, the child dissipates his forces.

But to be a parent or teacher in a Michaelic age still means to set boundaries for the young child. Boundaries give safety, security, assurance, and confidence—all of which the young child needs.

It is the quality of the boundary that must now be different than those set in a Gabrielic Age. Today, the setting of boundaries must come out of the consciousness of the individual adult and no longer from tradition, or from the guidelines of a particular group. This is difficult. Is it not easier for us either to give Sam a free rein, to let him be his own master, or to sit on him? Instead, to be truly modern adults means that we learn to discriminate what our priorities are and make decisions for the children.

Of course this is a challenge in that I, the teacher, make blunder after blunder. But I have Steiner's insights to help me—and he repeatedly stresses the importance of a rhythmical life, a rhythmical education—and, secondly, I sooner or later begin to feel that the other side of this challenge of self-reliance is joy—the joy of autonomy, the joy of carrying responsibility. One more word about the kind of boundary the young child is looking for in this, his chosen age of incarnation. It is that he needs boundaries that gradually grow wider, boundaries that can be supportive but not restrictive.

So, what does it mean for the young child to live his karma of being modem? What does it mean to be a member of the Michaelic Age as a young child? It means, in the first place, to find and develop courage and confidence in himself. It means to find and develop confidence in people and human existence, to find and develop courage for the future. Courage and confidence are born out of boundaries consciously set by parents and teachers. If a child was shaped and formed in some such way by parents and teachers, then in adulthood she is likely to have the strength and skill—physical, social and moral strength and skills—to shape and form life on her own responsibility.

Before I come to the question of the personal karma of the young child, I want to turn to the parent. Again a story: A young woman was in the fifth month of expecting her second child: "This is a very different pregnancy. It is all fiery. The other one was watery." The little one was then born on Midsummer Day. This and other stories can attest to the relationship between mother and child during pregnancy. Steiner describes the following: When the Ego is in the spirit-world and is face to face with creator beings, the Ego also decides who are to be the parents. Then the parents descend. Later the spirit-child sees the parents, is reminded of the three-way decision, and conception takes place. Steiner describes—and modem psychology and embryology give concrete examples—how during embryonic life the mother is in communication with the incarnating soul. She perceives something of the child, e.g., the name: "It's going to be Robert." Steiner speaks of a spirit bonding. Still later, but before birth, the spirit-child has a preview of his life and the mother shares in it. When I read the autobiography of Gerald Moore, the pianist and accompanist of all the great singers of his time, I wondered why his mother had given him a certain push into his career. Had there arisen and lived in her a broad outline of the child's destiny?

That the mother intuits the child's karma can arouse positive or negative feelings in her. What if they are negative? Can it be that during the years prior the arrival of the child the parents did not shape and form their lives consciously? The mother says, "What, I am housebound? I never expected that!" The father says, "What, I have to be up in the night? I never expected that!" And is it not another form of immaturity of the parent when the child can never do anything right, when the parents always appear to be dissatisfied? There seems to be a conflict, the conflict of what the parents want the child to be and what the child in reality is. And what if this goes further and the parent does not approve of the child's destiny?

A conversation might help, when I, a friend of the family, try to lift the parent out of experiencing a screaming child. I try to release the mother from experiencing defiance, and again, defiance. I try to interest her in her early experience: "How did you feel when Richard smiled at you for the first time?" Then I might try to go back to her earlier experiences: "How did you come to the name of the child? What did you experience during pregnancy, what thoughts did you have?" Gently, we try to recognize the intimacy of the soul-to-soul in pregnancy. This recognition aims at a kind of listening.

I have come to the last point: personal karma. Two stories: Marie was four years old when she came into the kindergarten. From the first day she showed intense fear at the least mention of lighting a candle. The teacher learned from the parents that the child had never experienced a fire and that she had always been healthy. She had a noticeably milky-white and velvety skin and showed a remarkable walk in that she neither dragged her feet upon the ground nor walked on her toes only. There seemed to be a certain balance between gravity and levity in posture and movements. She was loved by children and adults and provided a focus in the room wherever she happened to be. Neither parent had learnt a second language nor been outside England. But when this first child was born they said, "We want her to have a French name." And so the little one was named Marie. It took teachers, with the help of the parents, over four years to transform Marie's crying and running away at the sight of the smallest flame into weeping, whimpering, turning her head, and on into looking at the candle and smiling. Today Marie is an actress. She chose a profession which asks of the person to enflame other personalities, to kindle and enliven other lives.

Rachel was a four-year-old when she came into the kindergarten. She was the third child in her family and came from a sheltered home in the country. Her eyes were set wide apart. In the kindergarten Rachel watched other children play. She might build herself a house out of two play stands and hang cloths over them, but then she would walk away again to watch other children in their activity. After about two weeks, the teacher and the parents noticed that Rachel moved her eyes and head in an unusual way. The family doctor diagnosed petit mal. We agreed on a pedagogical therapy of singing and music around and with the child, and also interesting her in an indirect way in the house she had built during playtime. By the time Rachel left school at the age of 18, she was an accomplished viola player who got into the Royal College of Music in London. Today she is working as a music therapist.

At this point I want to recall another suggestion of Steiner's. For me it is an admonition: "Do not interfere with the will of the child." Why? Because in his will, in his unconscious, lies his karma, and in karma freedom must reign. Is the previously mentioned statement of Steiner's, "The teacher continues the work of the creator beings," compatible with this statement, "Do not interfere with the will of the child?" I suggest the two statements are compatible because I must not interfere with the will of the child, must not break his will, as so often happened in the last century. It behooves me to recognize the karmic intentions of the child. Once I have recognized them, I can consciously work for karma. Then the teacher becomes a person who removes obstacles, and who creates opportunities so that the karmic intentions of the child can come out to the fullest degree.

Let me summarize a few guidelines and practices. I like to call them the disciplines of adults who are intent on helping the child out of his past and into his future:

1. That we be observant of bodily features;
2. That we be observant of developmental features;

3. That we be observant of psychological peculiarities;
4. That we do well to study Steiner's karma lectures;
5. That we do well to become aware of human history, to gauge the state of a soul like Marie's. I often wondered whether this excessive fear of fire was not a subconscious memory of her death in a former incarnation.

And so to conclude: In education parent and teacher are encouraged to make themselves sensitive to karmic differences and to karmic needs. Thereby, we open the way for the young child to become fully capable within the limits of her or his karma, and we endeavor to educate human beings who are capable of fulfilling the plan of creator beings, capable of answering the expectations of Michael.

Margaret Meyerkort guided a Waldorf kindergarten training in Gloucester, England for many years and lectured and gave courses in early childhood education throughout the English-speaking world. She is the author of the Wynstones collection of books, including Spring, Summer, Winter, Fall, Gateways *and* Spindrift.

Walking and the Incarnation of Destiny

Joan Almon

We can all picture what it is like to watch a young toddler who is just beginning to walk. One's heart is warmed at the sight. The legs are spread wide and the gait rolls a bit as the child seeks balance. There is many a bump as the child falls down and rises again to its feet. We may also feel a sense of wonder, for there are great mysteries hidden in this seemingly simple deed.

If we look into the far past of mankind's development and ask at what point did the human being stand upright and walk, then Rudolf Steiner points us to ancient Lemuria. Before this, we moved in the horizontal position like the animal kingdom does today. It required the incarnation of the ego in the earth stage of development for human beings to stand upright and walk and this was a great moment in human evolution. Its implications for the destiny of the human being were so great that it drew the attention of Ahriman and Lucifer, who wished to interfere with this important step in human development. They would have loved to enter in at this moment, Ahriman pulling us far down into the physical earthly nature. Perhaps there would have been no full uprightness; or, in Lucifer's case, lifting us so that our feet would not fully touch the earth—not allowing us to embrace earthly incarnation. These were the two great dangers that faced mankind as walking began. Steiner says in his lecture entitled *The Pre-Earthly Deeds of the Christ*, that a similar threat arose from Ahriman and Lucifer when we learned to speak in the early days of Atlantis and when we learned to think in the late days of Atlantis. These were three great moments in evolution and three great dangers. Steiner goes on to say that the Christ Being came to the aid of humanity each time. The same Being, who later appeared in the body of Jesus, intervened on behalf of mankind from the spiritual heights, holding Ahriman and Lucifer at bay, so that mankind could walk, could talk and could think.

This protection by the Christ Being is reenacted in the life of every individual. In the first three years, while the child masters walking, talking and thinking, the spiritual world gathers around in protection. Ahriman and Lucifer are held at bay. Thus when we see a young child take its first steps we are right in feeling a sense of joy and wonder, for there are great mysteries which stand behind the outwardly simple deed of walking.

Turning our sights away from the spiritual history of mankind to the children before us, we can see a series of stages. When we watch the child gain mastery of its physical body in the first year we see a fascinating pattern of development emerge. Emmi Pikler, a physician who had a baby center in Hungary, did intensive observation of children learning to walk and wrote on this subject. Her books have not been translated into English yet.

She observed that children all follow a basic pattern of movement which eventually leads them towards crawling, standing upright, walking, climbing, et cetera. The young child should not be rushed or hindered in the mastery of these movements.

Another active observer of the young child is Joan Salter, an anthroposophical nurse in Australia who founded the Gabriel Baby Centre, a type of well–baby clinic. In her book, *The Incarnating Child,* she described certain archetypal gestures she observed in children's movement during that first year. From early on, when the infant is on its back asleep, its little arms stretch up on either side of its head, looking like the first two little leaves which spring from the stem of a sprouting plant. If the child is ill, the little arms drop to the side like the leaves of an ailing plant. One could say this is the plant stage in human movement.

A next stage in movement is the fish stage when the child lies on its tummy and lifts its legs. Often the feet are together looking like a fish tail. In a next stage the child lifts the legs as well as the upper chest and arms, so that it looks like it is going to fly. This is the bird stage. In the reptile stage, the child squirms across the floor on its belly, and in the four-legged quadruped stage, it rises on all fours and begins to crawl. At last comes the human stage, when the child pulls itself up onto two legs and begins to walk. It has worked its way through the kingdoms of nature into the human stage. In her book, Joan Salter also likened these stages to the great geological periods of the earth.

Another picture emerges from Karl Koenig's book The *First Three Years,* where he speaks of certain instincts in the infant for crawling, standing upright and walking. These instincts exist and can be activated by touching the feet in certain ways. In this regard the infant resembles the animal kingdom, for the newborn animals have strong instincts for standing up and walking. Many can do it in the first hours after birth. In the human being, however, a different process takes place. We do not master walking out of instinct like the animals.

We lose these instincts by the time we are several months old, and we then go through a process of learning to walk. We are helped in learning to walk by the spiritual world, in the form of the archai. We are helped by human beings through our gift of imitating their capacity to walk. And we are helped by the growing strength of the ego within, which wants to get up and walk, leaving the realm of the animals behind.

The deed of walking has many aspects, and each has implications for our whole life. To begin with, walking requires the activation of our will which is so closely related to our limbs. The development of will is of special interest to the kindergarten teacher and can be illustrated with a series of examples. A six–month–old, named Gordon, was observed over a period of a month as he tried to turn from his back to his stomach. Again and again and again he worked at this until at last he accomplished it. He never showed signs of frustration and seemed undaunted by the hundreds of times he failed to turn over. He kept trying until at last he succeeded, and then began to work on the next type of movement.

A similar focus of will was seen in a four-and-a-half-year-old girl named Ivana. She came to kindergarten one Monday and announced that she could tie a bow. She demonstrated it with great ease and skill. Her teacher wondered how she had come to learn this complicated task which is usually not mastered at such a young age. The week before she had shown no interest in tying bows at all. When the mother was asked how this had come about, she laughed and described Ivana's weekend. For two days she pretended she was going to a birthday party and folded up every bit of paper she could find in the house. From her mother's yarn basket she cut strings for wrapping up her "birthday packages." Again and again and again she tied bows, making a total of perhaps sixty or seventy such packages. It would have been terrible to have "assigned" her such a task, but out of the spirit of play and the power of her own will forces she took it on for herself, bringing forth a skill that was ready to be born.

As a next stage of development of the will forces, a picture was given of a six–year–old boy who built himself a car in the kindergarten and now was trying to find a way to steer it. The car was made of two stumps that had been turned on their side with a wide board lying across them. If he straddled the board and pushed with his feet he could make the car roll a bit, but he could not steer it this way. On this particular day he wanted to find a way to steer it and spent forty–five minutes trying to tie a rope onto the stumps and onto the board in such a way as to connect the two and maneuver it. Again and again he tried it, first one way and then another. At last he gave up, and with a shrug dropped his rope and went off to play with a friend. One felt he had learned as much from a seeming failure as he would have from a success. One day he would realize that an axle and a drive shaft are needed for this step, which a simple rope could not accomplish. In the meantime, he had fully directed his will to the task and seemed not at all frustrated by his inability to make it work.

Not long after this, at a point when he was showing strong signs of first–grade–readiness, the same boy had a conversation with his teacher. She was churning butter and was at the point of paddling the butter to separate off the buttermilk. He was watching her and noted that although the cream had been white when it entered the churn, the butter was now yellow. "Why?" he asked. The teacher told him she did not know, but had always wondered about this change in color. Simply wondering was not enough for him. He seemed to gather up his will forces and direct them towards his thinking. One could almost feel the wheels of thought going around. He stood by the teacher for several moments with a look of deep concentration on his face. He then brightened up and announced, "I know why. You see, the cream came from a cow and the cow ate grass and the grass was green. Green is made up of blue and yellow, and that is where the yellow came from." Having concluded this he went off to his next activity, leaving his teacher in amazement. Her amazement grew even deeper some time later when she repeated this story to a group of parents and one, who had milked many cows, said, "He's absolutely right. In the summer when the cows eat grass the butter from their cream is yellow, while in winter when they eat hay the butter turns white. This occurs because the grass contains carotene, the same substance which makes carrots orange." Many old-fashioned farmers' wives added natural yellow coloring to their winter butter to give it a bright summery look. One finds a description of this process in one of Laura Ingalls Wilder's books.

When this story was told to a Waldorf high school mathematics teacher, he remarked that it is this same force of will in the thinking that is so necessary for a student to do well in math. One sees how some students have great difficulties penetrating a problem with their will forces, while others apply their will with great success. Doing well in math is not only
a question of native ability. It is also a question of directed, focused will in the thinking. Thus, in this way, will evolves from the

earliest movements of infancy, through the play of childhood, and takes its place in adult activity in human thought.

Another aspect of walking is the upright nature of the human being. We tend to take this for granted, but it is a very significant step that carries us out of the instinctual, animal realm and into the human sphere. Yet many children display a strong wish to remain in the animal sphere in their kindergarten play. What should one do for such a child? Some teachers forbid all forms of animal play in the kindergarten in order to help the children play out human roles. Others allow all forms of animal play but often complain of how wild the kindergarten becomes and of how one feels the mood has sunken in an unpleasant way. One way was described in which the children may play animal roles, but only domesticated animals, those who live in relationship to human beings such as cats and dogs or farm animals. "Wild animals are for outside," but outside the children usually forget about them and do not engage in animal play. When one allows animal play, then one needs to observe the children who are drawn to it in order to decide if it is a healthy stage of play or whether a child is stuck in animal play and needs help to emerge from it into human play. Two examples were given.

In one, a five-year-old was described who had a very strong stubborn streak in her. She was unusually independent and at times uncooperative. Because of this, it was difficult to fully relate to her in the kindergarten. At one point she became ill with whooping cough and was home for a month. When she returned she seemed to have outgrown her extreme stubbornness. She was in a sweeter place, though physically a bit weak and vulnerable. Around this time she began to take animal roles in a farm play which the children repeated over a period of time. She was usually a sheep or a cow and liked to be near people who would care for her. When this phase ended she rose to her feet again and began to show much more care towards others. The sweet side of her nature began to emerge more and more. Her fierce independence and stubbornness, that had often alienated her from other children, was tempered by good will and concern for others. In her case, playing animal seemed to have been a temporary backward step which did her much good.

In another case, however, a boy who was always nervous and tense tended to play animal roles nearly all the time. His animals tended not to live closely with human beings, but were often alone and sometimes rather wild. Out of himself he rarely stayed on his feet in a human role for the whole of playtime. In this case it seemed he was "caught" in the horizontal and needed help to come more fully up into the vertical. The teacher chose to intervene and would frequently take him by the hand when he wanted to engage in animal play and bring him to a work activity or help him build a human house for himself. Gradually he spent less and less time as an animal, and also became a much more harmonious child. He was the child who, two years later, gave the wonderful explanation about the yellow butter. In his case, helping him move away from animal play towards human play seemed to have been a helpful and necessary step.

Another aspect of walking is the freeing of the hands. Once the child stands erect it no longer needs its hands for movement. What does this signify for the human being? We speak of animals or other lowly beings as "creatures", something less than human. Someone using the full capacities of being human is a "creator." Similar sounding words but with such different meanings. When the child stands upright and has access to its hands, it leaves the world of the creature and joins forces with the world of the creator. A whole new element begins to enter the human soul. For some children this transition seems difficult. They enter the kindergarten and look as if they do not know what to do with their hands, which seem to dangle lifelessly at their sides. Or they use their hands to behave in animal-like ways, pinching like a crab, scratching like a cat, hitting like a bear. Their hands need to be brought up into the human realm of creation. All kindergarten children need to see the healthy work which human hands can do, but such children may need extra help to interest their hands in creative, human activity. It is not only the creative work of painting, drawing or modeling which is necessary for the children, but the daily work of table setting, dishwashing, and handwork which helps children more fully experience the realm of being human.

When our hands are freed, when they can be lifted up high, something of the divine enters into us. An element of God the Creator becomes awake in our being. At the end of the Oberufer Paradise Play, this is depicted beautifully. The devil's chains fall from Adam and Eve, and Adam is free to raise up his arms. Then God speaks and says, "See now, this Adam such wealth has won Like to a God he is become, Knowledge he has of evil and good, He can lift up his hand on high, Whereby he liveth eternally."

This beautiful passage also points to another aspect of human uprightness and walking, that of knowing good and evil. We can call this the area of human morality, and can consider what is meant when we say a person is *upright*. The children look to us for guidance in the human, moral realm as well as in the other realms discussed, and each teacher must think through how to bring this realm to life in the kindergarten. We do not preach or moralize with young children, but yet a moral tone needs to be established so that the children can live together in peace.

Another aspect of walking pertains to the destiny of the individual. In *The Waking of the Human Soul and the Forming of Destiny*, Rudolf Steiner says, "The primary measure of destiny is expressed in the learning to walk." (p. 11) How are we to understand this? It might first seem to us that all children walk the same in the beginning, but on closer observation we see significant differences in the early steps of a child. As kindergarten teachers we do not have many opportunities to observe this phase of development, but those who work with children in the first three years may note these differences and develop a sense of their significance.

In his lectures on karmic relationships, Rudolf Steiner gives another picture of the importance of walking to individual karma. He often traces a person's past life by noting how they walk in this lifetime. In this regard he speaks of his own geometry teacher, a man who had a profound impact on him when he was a student. He describes the man as he knew him in this lifetime, a man who was a great geometrician but whose thinking did not go beyond the bounds of geometry into mathematics as a whole. Even within geometry, he was not open to the many changes that were then taking place in that field. One gets the impression that his thinking was narrowly circumscribed, but within those limits his thinking was profound. Steiner then speaks of how this man was incarnated with a clubfoot. He often thought of his teacher, and of the significance of his physical condition and then began to understand a past life which his teacher had shared with the individuality who later became the English poet Byron. Byron, too, was born with a clubfoot. In a previous incarnation these two men had known each other and had set out on a great spiritual mission together. They were not successful in this mission, and although Rudolf Steiner does not spell out the picture in detail, one gets the feeling that the cut-off mission of the past mirrors itself in the physical condition of the next incarnation.

Can such pictures speak to us as kinder garten teachers who are trying to help the children meet their own karmic situations? Most of us do not have these insights into our past lives, but we do have opportunities to help the children with meeting their destiny in the present. Often one gets the feeling that a child's way is blocked—that something stands in the way of moving forward to meet his or her destiny. One wants to help, but how? The young child in the first seven years lives so strongly in the realm of movement that often it is through movement that the blockage can be removed or at least minimized. When the child shows a greater difficulty, curative eurythmy can be a great help in removing hindrances from a child's path. In simpler cases, the activities that arise in the kindergarten can clear the way. A few examples were given.

A little girl, age five, was described as being very sweet and very good, but perhaps too good. Of such children, Rudolf Steiner said to be careful, for the spirit does not flow strongly enough in them. She participated in the kindergarten but not with the enthusiasm and joy that one expects from a healthy child. At times she would sit alone and look quite sad and heavy-hearted. Towards the end of winter there was a large snowstorm, and when the school's parking lot was plowed, a large mound of snow was pushed to the end of the lot. When all the snow from the playground had melted, the children were allowed to play on this mound. She wanted to play there with the other children, but had great difficulty walking on the snow that was very uneven. She was encouraged to persist; and every day for a week she struggled across the snow, backwards and forwards, until at last she could walk across it with ease. She had found a new form of balance in her walking, and in herself as well, for after this she was a much more enthusiastic participant in the kindergarten.

In another case, some boys between six and seven years old were growing disenchanted with the kindergarten. They were at a difficult stage of first–grade–readiness and seemed blocked in finding a new relationship to the kindergarten. On a rainy day, the teacher set up a "circus" for them with a high wire act, consisting of an eight–inch wide board suspended between two tables. She suggested they walk across it thinking that, as they were first–grade–ready, they should have sufficient balance for such a task. They were afraid, however, and did not trust themselves to do it, but she offered her hand that they held onto with all their might. After a few crossings they began to realize they could do it and held her hand much more loosely. Then they crossed without holding on. They began to grow very confident and started to hop across, to walk with their eyes closed, to walk across backwards, et cetera. After this day of circus play, it was as if an inner blockage had been removed from them, and they showed fresh enthusiasm for all the kindergarten had to offer them.

A final aspect of walking which was included in the lecture pertained to the question of the future destiny of mankind. In which direction is mankind walking? Who will guide our steps along the path of the future? In the lecture *Easter: The Mystery of the Future* (April 13, 1908), Steiner describes the spiritual path of mankind in this way. "In the ancient past mankind lived very closely with the gods. In Atlantis, the realm of the gods was the reality for mankind, even as today mankind is at home with the plants and animals. At that time, the physical world was hazy and unclear to mankind, but the spiritual world was very clear. Gradually, mankind's consciousness descended away from the heavenly and towards the earthly. At the time of Egypt, for example, the thrust of spiritual life was to bring consciousness down to earth. One feels this in the Egyptian temples where one enters first into an open-air courtyard, then an enclosed courtyard, then into one room after another, each growing smaller in size. One has the sense of penetrating inward to the center and being brought down. What a difference this is in contrast to entering a Gothic cathedral. The whole thrust of the cathedral is upward and the human spirit rises with it. In the Egyptian temple, mankind's spirit was still in the process of incarnating, whereas after the time of the Christ, the direction of the human spirit is upwards again.

Now we are on the journey up, and Rudolf Steiner says much progress will be made in this age of the consciousness soul, a two thousand-year period that began in the fifteenth century. In particular, he says that the twentieth century will be a critical time for mankind's journey. At this time, we begin to separate ourselves from the dense consciousness of the physical and turn our attention upwards. The etheric body of the modern human beings begins to loosen itself from the dense physical world and with it the consciousness begins to loosen. This is not an easy process for all human beings. Some are so attached to the physical that they cling too hard and are fearful of moving towards the spiritual. One result of this is the growth of pathological fears suffered by so many modern human beings. It is important that modern human beings find their way along this new path towards the spirit. "If he [mankind] has lost consciousness of the spiritual world, has come to believe that life in the physical body and things to be seen in the physical world are the only realities, then for all ages of time he must dangle, as it were, in mid-air. He will have lost his bearings in the spiritual world and will have no ground under his feet. He will be threatened, in this condition, with what is known as the *spiritual death*. That is the death in the spiritual world. It is the doom which threatens men if, before passing again into the spiritual worlds, they fail to bring with them any consciousness of those worlds." (*The Festivals and Their Meaning*, pp. 200-201)

Fortunately we have not been abandoned on this journey. The Christ being came to mankind's aid when he first learned to walk and was threatened by the presence of Ahriman and Lucifer. His presence on the earth marked a new direction for mankind, and His working with the hierarchies aids every child as it learns to walk anew. He prepared to help us walk along this new path towards the spirit. Of the Christ's new task Steiner says, "He will not only be comforter, but the one who goes before us. In the future Christ's being will permeate all knowledge, all art, all life. His presence lights our path into the future."

Joan Almon was co-founder of the Waldorf Early Childhood Association of North America, the General Secretary of the Anthroposophical Society, and is the U.S. Coordinator of the Alliance for Childhood.

Continuing the Work of the Hierarchies in the Age of the Etheric Christ

Werner Glas

There is a great variety in the way we, as educators, approach our work with the young child. An imp might enter and say, "Oh, see, we can do whatever we want in the kindergarten. Just see how differently these teachers all do it!" But our differences have grown out of our meditative work and our study. Such inner work gives one the right to be original and different. We must sharpen our responsibility to work out of the central impulse of anthroposophy. We need to work with a willingness to serve and protect the young child, to further his right to survive as a spiritual being. It is not easy to be born into the present time. Until 1879, we were only experiencing the preparatory stage of materialism, its embryonic period. Now the real period of materialism is beginning and will be with us for two hundred to three hundred years.

In the movie *Short Circuit,* a robot is struck by lightning and is greatly changed. He displays wonder and awe and imitates a butterfly flying across a meadow. A scientist decides the robot has become human. The mistaking of machines for humans is symptomatic of our times and began with the robot in *Star Wars*. It is a sign that our sense of ego is blunted. We cannot distinguish between that which is truly human and that which is not. We must learn to find the human element so that we can better communicate with the parents, not only about problems, but also about their solutions. It is not enough to look for symptoms of materialism; we need to also look for symptoms of hope.

On March 15, 1906, in Berlin, Rudolf Steiner offered this distinction between individuality and personality:

> Today one easily confuses the concepts of individuality and personality. The Individuality is the eternal that which carries through from earth life to earth life. Personality is that which the human being within one life brings towards all that forms his or her development. If we wish to study the individuality, we must look to the very basis of the human soul; if we wish to study the personality, we must see how the essential kernel of the human being comes to expression. The kernel of being, the essential essence, is born into a people, into a profession.

This is all decided—or personalized— by the inner being. When a human being is at a lower stage of development, one will notice little of his or her inner work because the mode of expression is taken from the folk. Those who are more evolved will find a way of expression, and gestures, that come from their inner life. The more the inner life of the human being can work on the outer, the more the human being develops. One could say in this way the individuality comes to expression in the personality. A marked personality will have a distinct character through gesture, through physiognomy, even through the way he or she works on the environment. Does this personality element become lost at the point of death for subsequent development? No, that is not so. Christianity knows quite exactly that this is not the case.

That which is understood as the resurrection of the body is nothing other than the maintenance of the personality in all subsequent incarnations. That which has been gained by the human being as a person, that "person–hood," is embodied in the individuality, and for that reason is carried on into following incarnations. If we have made something of our body that has its own special character, then the forces that work to bring this about will resurrect. As much as we have worked on ourselves, as much as we have made of ourselves, is not lost for us.

Where is the unique kernel of our being carried? It is carried in the realm of the angels. For the angel, the I of the human is what the physical body is for the individual. Our walking, talking, and thinking are the lowest members of the angel's being. In the angel, all the other hierarchies are reflected. Through the angel they all work into our I. We seek ways to work more closely with the angels.

Here is an example: I went on a whale-watching expedition, which has become a very popular activity in America. During this summer 200,000 people went whale watching. Fleets of boats go out and the guides get to know the whales individually. Seeing these whales awakens sympathy in people. It "rings a bell" in the unconscious realm of the soul, in a place where memories of Atlantis lie. For some people seeing the whales changes their dream life in the following days and affects them in positive ways. To get in touch with these realms of one's own soul life can give new possibilities for working with the angels.

Rudolf Steiner spoke of the differences between imagination and fantasy. They are not the same. At the end of *Study of Man* he gives a three-line verse that begins "Imbue thyself with the power of fantasy." It does not say with the power of imagination. The depth of that difference becomes apparent in the following quotation, taken from the lecture entitled "The Human Being in the World of the Hierarchies" (October 22, 1921) in Volume III of *Anthroposophy as Cosmosophy*.

> The human being has a singular, an individual relationship to his angel. That relationship expresses itself in two ways. It expresses itself in inner experience when the human being allows himself to go beyond himself, to go outside himself from within. . . in ordinary life, however, as this is an intimate matter, something luciferic easily mixes into the process. Nevertheless, the human being can go beyond himself as a soul experience and, to a certain extent, experience something objective in fantasy. In many ways fantasy is very creative, but individually creative, like language. And, basically, the activity of fantasy is the basis of language.
>
> Just as people frequently only experience something abstract in language, just as the genius of language, which is an archangel, cannot always spread its wings, so the luciferic weaving in fantasy obstructs the perception and makes fantasy fantastic. In actuality an angel slips through the life of the individual while he lives in fantasy.
>
> When an individual lives in fantasy, the angels enter the life of the individual. The same force that shapes the brain in the first years, later enters the human being as fantasy. This is really the working of the angels in human life.
>
> When a child observes the world, he becomes

the world. This is the same process we experience between death and rebirth. In *Leaves of Grass,* Walt Whitman speaks of the child going forth every day, and everything the child beholds becomes part of him.

> There was a child went forth everyday, / and the first object he looked upon, that object he became, / and that object became part of him for the day or a certain part of the day, / Or for many years or stretching cycles of years.

This is the same process as the merging of spirits in the spiritual world. We do not "meet" a spiritual being; we become the spiritual being, we merge with it. We then carry this capacity for merging into our incarnation on earth and experience it during early childhood.

During the Basel course on May 10, 1920[2], Rudolf Steiner made reference to play. He differentiates between play in the first seven years and between seven and fourteen. The fruits of the first play only appear in the twenties, when the ego is born deeply into the human being. "The force that is applied in the child's play reappears in the twenty-first or twenty-second year as the intellect, now independently collecting its experience in life." The early effects of fantasy and play appear again in the thirties when the consciousness soul becomes active.

This transformation of play and fantasy forces is explained by a remarkable set of concepts, which at first seem very simple, but which in actuality are not simple at all. We have to work with these ideas. In 1819 Goethe wrote the following in an article entitled "Sight from a Subjective Point of View:"

> I have the gift that when I shut my eyes and lower my head and think of a flower in the center of my organ of seeing, the image does not remain in its first form for a moment; rather, does the form fall apart. From its innermost aspect new flowers develop, also with green leaves. These are not natural flowers but fantasy flowers—like the rosettes created by a sculptor. It was impossible to fix the fountain-like creation in a static position. The process lasted as long as I wanted it to last. It did not fade nor did it intensify.

Christopher Fry offers a similar picture in "The Lady's Not for Burning" when he refers to seeds and says, "I hold in my hand a generation of roses." The seed is the involution, the future flower the evolution; one is the contraction, the other is the expansion. Here we have karmic situation and karmic response. But not everything in life is the result of karmic necessity. Rudolf Steiner says, "Create out of the nothing." This pertains to the power of fantasy, to the shaping of the future.

The model for our physical body was begun on Ancient Saturn, but it must also be reworked. Added to it has been the model of the etheric body of the Christ. Rudolf Steiner said that between the Twelfth and Fifteenth Centuries, the model of the astral body of Jesus became available for a number of incarnating human souls, such as Francis of Assisi.

Now there is a renewal of all that carries the I. Christianity has reached the point where it can go from the ordinary I, the walking, talking, thinking I, to the Pauline I, where we can say, "Not I, but the Christ in me." Inasmuch as we stimulate the forces of fantasy in the young child, later, when the consciousness soul develops, this step becomes more possible. Rudolf Steiner has said that joy in the first seven years is the basis for the consciousness soul. The forces of fantasy can transform one and enable one to overcome egotism. When Rudolf Steiner gave the *Teacher's Imagination,* he gave the image of the chalice of courage. It is Michael who brings us the courage we need to overcome the materialism of the age.

1. Rudolf Steiner's use of the word *Genius* accords with its Latin meaning which refers to the spirit of an individual or place or, as in this case, one's spiritual or angelic companion.
2. *Essentials of Education,* Rudolf Steiner, Anthroposophic Press, NY, 1997.

Werner Glas was the founder and director of the Waldorf Institute/Sunbridge College, and was a founding member of the board of WECAN. He was instrumental in the founding of many Waldorf schools and kindergartens in North America.

Early Childhood and the Consciousness Soul

Joan Almon

When Rudolf Steiner spoke of the human being, he not only described body, soul, and spirit, but spoke of three levels for each. Thus within the body are the physical, etheric, and astral bodies; within the soul are the sentient, intellectual, and consciousness souls, and within the spirit are spirit self, life spirit, and spirit man (also called the spirit body). This is described in detail in the opening chapter of Steiner's *Theosophy,* as well as in his introductory booklet, *The Education of the Child.*

Particularly important for modern human beings is the development of the consciousness soul. This is the newest aspect of the human soul, the two lower soul forces having been developed in earlier epochs. Our current epoch, which began with the Renaissance and will last about two thousand years, provides the conditions under which humanity as a whole can develop this higher soul capacity. The consciousness soul carries a full awareness of the soul nature of the human being and also provides a bridge to understanding the spiritual. In the future, humanity as a whole will be able to develop spiritual capacities in a much fuller way than is possible today. Nevertheless, every human being willing to do so is able to develop soul and spiritual capacities to a large extent, especially if the individual's upbringing and education are supportive of it.

Through a beautiful pattern of development, the three seven-year phases of the first twenty-one years are *transformed* into the three soul phases that develop between ages twenty-one and forty-two. Rudolf Steiner indicates that the growth forces and experiences of the first seven years play a vital part in the development of the consciousness soul between ages thirty-five and forty-two. The school years, between seven and fourteen, serve as a basis for the development of the mind or intellectual soul between twenty-eight and thirty-five, and adolescence, between fourteen and twenty-one, prepares for the development of the sentient soul between twenty-one and twenty-eight. Later, these soul and body forces are again transformed into the three phases of spiritual development between forty-two and sixty-three. My focus here will be on the impact that the first seven years of life have on the development of the consciousness soul between thirty-five and forty-two.

When one looks at the whole of human development in this way, then one can say that in the first twenty-one years the human being is concentrating especially on the body; in the next twenty-one years on the soul, and in the following twenty-one years on the spirit. In the first twenty-one years one more or less follows the pattern of physical development implanted in one. This development is influenced by environment, education and other factors, but there is little the child can do to influence its own physical development. This development works in accordance with laws implanted within the child. Since the ego is not yet fully incarnated, there is less possibility for individual initiative and freedom.

After the birth of the ego around age twenty-one, the individual has the chance to transform the growth forces of the first twenty-one years into the three soul aspects. This is a challenge and is influenced in part by how well the development occurred in the first twenty-one years. If the Ego finds itself with an undernourished physical body, a weakened etheric, or a chaotic astral, then the task of developing the soul forces becomes much more difficult than it would otherwise be.

As the soul forces develop, one sees that the greatest challenge is in developing the consciousness soul, for it is such a new member of the human being. Humanity as a whole developed the sentient soul in the Egyptian epoch and the mind soul in the Greco-Roman epoch. Now, in the modern epoch (which began in the 1400s) humanity is developing the consciousness soul: the vital gateway to spiritual awareness.

One might wonder: Why should it be so difficult to develop the consciousness soul? After all, we have already experienced nearly six hundred years of the consciousness soul epoch. Until the beginning of this century, however, two situations existed that hindered the development of the consciousness soul. They are now removed, and humanity is in a more active, intense period of development. One hindrance was the Kali Yuga, the Dark Age that lasted for five thousand years, ending only in 1899. During this period, humanity was increasingly separated from the forces of spirituality and light. Some strong individuals stood out and reached toward the light, but, in general, humanity felt the strength of spiritual darkness. Now humanity as a whole can experience the light of spirituality much more fully, and one is continually astonished at how widespread a basic recognition of spirituality is becoming.

The second change was the beginning of the Michaelic period in 1879. The Archangel Michael strengthens individuality, a quality much needed by the consciousness soul. During the first few hundred years of the consciousness soul epoch, the Archangel Gabriel took the lead in guiding humanity. Gabriel is the Archangel associated with birth, childhood, and family. Under his influence all relations based on blood ties are especially strong. Under the Archangel Michael, blood ties become less important as individuals seek a new, more conscious basis for community building.

These two changes have allowed humanity to work much more intensively on the consciousness soul during the past hundred years. As kindergarten teachers, we need to take seriously the relationship that Rudolf Steiner indicated between the first seven years of life and the years thirty–five and forty–two, when individuals are working to develop the consciousness soul. If the difficulties of the first seven years are too great, then the individual can feel trapped in the lower soul bodies. He or she can find it very difficult to come into the new realm of the consciousness soul, and will find it nearly impossible to move beyond it into spiritual realms after age forty–two. Here one sees the problem of "mid-life crisis." This can be a tragic turning away from higher development of the soul and spirit, and a return to the familiar space of lower development. One grabs hold of youth and the sentient soul, or builds a fortress around oneself, where the intellectual or mind soul alone is cultivated.

So much of human development hangs on the question of whether human beings can take the next step into the consciousness soul and then onward into the spirit. Because this step is so important, the opposing forces of Lucifer and Ahriman do all they can to hold humanity back. We can see this throughout human life, but their influence is especially marked in the first seven years. If the little child's development is seriously disturbed, the individual will find it much harder to break through later into higher soul and spirit realms. One could say that tampering with early childhood is the most efficient method for Lucifer and Ahriman to work if they want to interfere with the soul-spiritual development of the human being. A little interference there, so that the child is prematurely hardened or kept too long in a soft, non-incarnated state, has tremendous consequences later.

One way the opposing forces work on young children is to awaken the nerve-sense system prematurely. Modern children are often very quick and conscious, but they have difficulty staying in touch with the more dream-like consciousness through which they can learn and grow so actively. This change can be seen in children's pictures. Traditionally, children all over the world have tended to the same motifs in approximately the same sequence. These pictures arose from the child's being in touch with its own growth forces, as is well described in Michaela Strauss's book on children's drawings. However, in the foreword, written in the 1970s, Strauss pointed out that children's drawings were undergoing a change. Children of that time were less able to draw the archetypal motifs than were children before World War II, whose pictures were collected by her father. She points out that the phenomena have remained the same, i.e., the developmental patterns have not changed, "but the child's unconscious perception of the laws of development of his own being—which are mirrored in his drawings—appears to have become weaker. Should this fact be seen in connection with the nervousness and over–stimulation of today?" (*Understanding Children's Drawings*, p. 11)

Today the situation has grown so severe that many children cannot draw the archetypal pictures at all. Their drawings are full of cars, machines, weapons, dinosaurs, or other motifs that seem to come from a more awakened relationship to the world and not from a dream-like relationship to their own inner growth forces. Helping children return to archetypal drawing is a challenge, for ultimately one needs to help them be less awake and more dream-like. It is generally not sufficient simply to tell them they cannot draw such and such a picture. Finding a way back to archetypal drawings is a question for all of us to research.

One also sees the attack on childhood through an increase in illnesses such as asthma and allergies. Children in the U.S., for example, are much more stressed and nervous today than in previous times. Government statistics show that during the past few decades children's health has deteriorated greatly. Previously, about one and one–half percent of American children were considered so handicapped that they could not participate in a normal way in school or in life, in general. That figure has now grown to about six and one–half percent, while among children from low-income households it is an alarming ten percent.

Childhood today is under an attack that young children do not have the forces to withstand. We, as adults, have the strength and must find ways to help protect the children. All children need this help so they can have a healthier childhood, but also so they can have a healthier adulthood, with the possibility of healthy growth in the soul-spiritual realms. Many children today show signs of having come to earth with a special connection to this age of the consciousness soul. Young though they are, one feels them shaping their own destiny. For example, I have met children who have decided to become vegetarians at the age of four or five. This is not a parental decision, for the parents are not vegetarians. It is as if the children feel this is what is needed if they are to grow and thrive in this lifetime.

On a journey to Asia, I met children who were making decisions regarding what language to speak that seemed somewhat independent of what they would normally do through imitation. For example, a family with four children spent three years in America. The older two children learned English in school, but the newborn twins were at home with their mother who spoke Thai to them. The family then returned to Thailand. It would have been most natural for the children to drop their English. Instead, they spoke only English to one another, and all four of them, even the little twins, were fluent speakers with almost perfect American accents. It was as if the children recognized that, as modern souls, they would need English as well as Thai, and they took it upon themselves to keep their English alive.

All children come to the world with their own intentions, which were formulated during the time before birth. More and more one meets children whose intention seems to be to care deeply for the earth and to be at home with all people. It is not far-fetched to think of these souls as working strongly with Michaelic impulses, or to see that they will work strongly with the consciousness soul. For their sake, as well as for the sake of all children, one needs to be strong in providing protection for children today. Otherwise a generation of strong individuals, who have much to offer to the earth and humanity, may find themselves too burdened and unable to accomplish what they have set out to do.

It is probably no coincidence that during this century, when early childhood is under such attack, kindergarten education has come to life. Previously, there was no need—not only because mothers were at home, but also because the wisdom of the home sufficed to protect young children. Now the attacks are greater, and the wisdom of the kindergarten is needed to strengthen the children. Rudolf Steiner must have foreseen this need, for he placed much emphasis on founding a kindergarten. It was a great disappointment to him that it was not possible to start the kindergarten work during his lifetime. At a teachers' conference he said, "We need kindergartens! We need kindergartens!" One can almost hear him pounding the table.

In the Waldorf kindergarten we have so many means of helping and healing children—through play, through the work of the adult, through music, verse and gesture, through the arts. One could look at every aspect of the Waldorf kindergarten and ask: "How does this help prepare the child for developing the consciousness soul? How does this provide healing and protection for the child today?"

Here we will focus on one aspect in relationship to the consciousness soul: the fairy tale. Fairy tales have much to tell us about the consciousness soul, and in their own way they provide a picture for the child to grow into. The consciousness soul lives at the boundary of soul and spirit. In the fairy tales, a common motif is the marriage of the masculine and the feminine, often in the form of prince and princess. This is generally understood to be a picture of the marriage of spirit with soul. In some fairy tales, the soul is enchanted or hidden away and waits for the spirit to come and awaken it. In other fairy tales, such as *The Seven Ravens,* the masculine, or spirit, is enchanted, and it is the striving of the soul or feminine element that breaks the enchantment. In the awakening of the consciousness soul, one also gets both pictures. Sometimes the soul is more active, sometimes the spirit, and the individual seeks a balance between them, so that spirit and soul can be wed within.

One fairy tale stands out as a wonderful picture of soul and spirit working together, a Zulu tale from South Africa called *The Winning of Kwelanga*. Kwelanga is the daughter of the Chief and thus a princess. It is time for her to wed, and the Chief tests each young man by giving certain tasks, which none of them can complete. Then Zamo hears of Kwelanga and wants to win her hand. His elderly parents try to dissuade him, pointing out that many have tried and failed. His response is, "I must whistle with my own mouth." He arrives at the village of the Chief, who is surprised to see him alone. "Where is your retinue?" he asks, and the boy answers, "Among my people it is the custom to do such things alone." Already one senses that here is a youth on the path towards the consciousness soul, which often demands that we stand as an individual and act alone.

When Zamo sees Kwelanga, he is more determined than ever to win her hand. She sees him as well, and wants him as her partner. The tasks he is assigned are impossible, but each time he is at the point of failing, a song is sung from afar and the task is accomplished. The third time this happens, Zamo sees Kwelanga and realizes that she has sung the songs. They go to her father, and when he sees that his daughter wants to marry Zamo, he agrees. In this story, the marriage of soul and spirit comes about because both are active and want the union. It is a beautiful story and suited for the kindergarten, especially when told in the latter part of the year when the oldest children are getting ready for first grade.

Fairy tales provide wonderful pictures that can live and grow in the children and help prepare them for the time when they may become inwardly active and seek the union of soul and spirit. Rudolf Steiner spoke of fairy tales as being a good angel that accompanies a child from birth onward. He also spoke of the importance of puppetry and marionette work, calling it a remedy for the ills of civilization. Fairy tales and puppetry are only two examples of the riches available in the Waldorf kindergarten. We have so many activities that lay a foundation so that later, in the time of developing the consciousness soul, there will not be hindrances, but rather a base of experience that can readily be transformed into this highest aspect of soul life.

Joan Almon is co-founder of the Waldorf Early Childhood Association of North America, the General Secretary of the Anthroposophical Society, and is the U.S. Coordinator of the Alliance for Childhood.

Threshold Experiences of Children and Adults

Helmut von Kügelgen

Let us take the picture of a boy, a child in the third grade, whose father is a physicist, mathematician, and Waldorf teacher. On the one hand this boy is very awake, with a great dexterity for everything technical. On the other hand the boy is also a dreamer. If one sees him in the woods one notices that he still lives with the elemental beings. The doll he has made in the handwork lessons is an absolutely alive being for him, he holds it tenderly and takes it with him to bed at night.

He is an example of how the present is continually in a process of transformation. What is the present? It cannot be grasped. When it begins, it comes towards us from the future. If we want to take hold of it, it is already past. It is part of the challenge of the consciousness soul always to be in the present. Just like the boy who at one moment is wide awake and in the next a dreaming being. The same is demanded from us adults—to be fully present in every moment.

The moment has neither a beginning nor an end. The only thing like it is eternity. To come into the present moment under the light of eternity—that is the law of transformation. We can ask ourselves: Which is the most important moment in my life, the most important book, or the most important person? It is always the book I am presently reading, the person I am just meeting, the moment in which I find myself. Presence is a word of the consciousness soul. It is a challenge of the time spirit, who stands before us in the image of Michael: evil under our feet, the radiance of the heavens above us, our gaze directed into the future, the past always behind us. Thinking about the past and the future are, however, also important in the spirit of the consciousness soul. The more we go back into the memory of our past, the closer we come to the moment of origin and to where we truly come from.

With the spirit-soul we come to the creator, God. I hold something in my hand and begin to think about it, I get in touch with the creator of what I hold in my hand. If we bring stones, shells, wood, and fruit into the kindergarten, they will always communicate to us something about the one who has created them. This applies in the same way to plastic toys. Here, too, we become connected with the creator of these things. The creators of these objects want to produce things that are as genuine as possible, yet there is always an element of deception involved. This creator also wants to make a large profit, and we connect ourselves with his attitude. In the small daily things, we can see the threshold that we cross with the consciousness soul, and if we awake our consciousness, we bring the children into contact with the creator.

The thoughts we have in such a situation are so important. They determine the mood, the spiritual atmosphere in which the children breathe. What is important when we speak to the children about the Christ child or St. Nicholas? The children of the consciousness soul age, whom I described as awake, soon find out that they believe in the Christ child only to please their parents. When we speak about the Christ child or St. Nicholas, it is important that we ourselves are inwardly connected with the reality of these beings and forces. The children of the consciousness soul age do not want to be deceived, and we should not pretend but be convinced of the reality of these beings.

We have found what is above all transformation, namely Christ.

Creator   Christ   Holy Spirit
Past → Present → Future
Transformation

The power of love and the strength of truth streaming from Him must not be violated.

It is characteristic that children nowadays are inhibited when they come to the part of the Christian Community Sunday service (offered at some Waldorf schools) where they say, "I will seek Him." Parents ask: "Is the child not overtaxed to say these words?" What can one answer? On the one hand they are right, that is to say, when they themselves no longer are seekers. But if they themselves do not cease to be seekers of God or Christ, one can speak to them precisely about this: that one always seeks into the future. If we look into the past we find the Creator. If we look into the future we find the Holy Spirit. Rudolf Steiner expressed this in the Foundation Stone Meditation. The Christ verse is in the middle, with the verses devoted to God and the Holy Spirit is on either side.

We turn towards the past and the Father God with gratitude and reverence. The present is protected and guided by Christ. We turn towards the Holy Spirit in the future through thoughts and aims that seek light. Whom do they implore? The future wants to become the light in our consciousness. This means we live with the Holy Spirit in a way that brings a feeling of the consciousness soul, which may be expressed as, "We have to conquer the future." In the past we find many wonderful experiences, ideas, and thoughts, but each idea needs the will of the future to be trans-formed into an ideal. If the will does not take hold of the idea, if we do not connect it with the future, then the idea weakens us. This can only be understood out of the consciousness soul: each idea that I do not lift up to the ideal is weakening my will.

Rudolf Steiner spoke about this when the first Waldorf School opened. He said that the person who loses the connection with his past and cannot see the Creator any longer becomes an atheist and, fundamentally, this is an illness. The person who does not carry the will of the future into the idea, who does not have a relationship with the Holy Spirit, becomes narrow-minded. But for the person who does not find the Christ this is a misfortune, a stroke of fate.

And what about the many people who do not find the Christ or reject him? At the moment of death they experience the image of the Ascension of Christ. They see him streaming into the sunlight, the light that exists for the whole of humanity, and they develop the yearning to find Christ in their next earthly life. It is the secret of our time that the connection to the spirit has been lost. The consciousness soul is also closely connected with the forces of evil. Therefore we have allowed for Lucifer and Ahriman, the two faces of evil, always to be present in the picture of the human being. The age of the consciousness soul demands us all to always look at the human being in a threefold way. Please take this as concretely and practically as possible. In fundamentalism we experience having one God only, not a Trinity, and the looking at the world in a twofold way, so that good and evil stand in polarity.

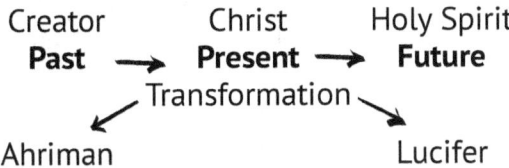

This threefold stance should be worked with as concretely and practically as possible. For, example, when within a school factions develop for or against someone or something, the issue is cast in a twofold light and becomes highly destructive. The more we are asked to decide either for or against, the more difficult it becomes in terms of a threefold dynamic, which would allow us to ask the question: How can this polarity be united on a higher level in love?

Let us glance into the width of history. The fourth cultural epoch (Greece and Rome) had the task of developing the intellectual, or mind soul. Its riddle was to deal inwardly with birth and death, as life after death become inaccessible to people living on earth at the time. Hades had become a land of shadows. The task of the fifth epoch, in which the consciousness soul is being developed, is dealing with the powers of evil. This can be ascertained through a shattering truth. The elemental beings responsible for birth and death, who hitherto were in the service of the Gods, we now meet from the outside. Birth as well as death is connected with the powers of destruction. The elemental beings at work in these processes were in earlier times led by the first of the Gods.

The law we find again and again in our education is that guidance must, after a certain time, lead to self-guidance. Freedom must be able to develop alongside love. The shattering truth is that elemental beings of destruction, the ahrimanic beings, now confront us from the outside. Rudolf Steiner prophesied before the time of radar, television and computers that these elemental beings will enter our time with an abundance of sublime inventions. He foretold the three forces of magnetism, electricity, and nuclear energy, of which these beings make use. This does not mean that these inventions should be avoided—they belong to the age of the consciousness soul—but it is most important that enough weight is put on the other side of the scales. It is a huge problem of balance; these sublime inventions need to be balanced by the faculty of imagination.

The inner secret is dealing with the forces of evil. How does one do that? Rudolf Steiner describes how all human beings have a leaning toward evil; we are capable of all crimes. What is required is the development of an inner path of schooling that enables us to be in command of this leaning. Then we can guide these forces in such a way that they become consciousness soul forces. In the sixth epoch, which begins at the end of the third millennium, these elemental beings will approach us ever more strongly. When Rudolf Steiner spoke about this theme he said that certain elemental beings were working towards the destruction of the earth. This destruction of the earth must not be prevented, but something indestructible needs to remain. Therefore he gives us a first means, which we must unfold more and more: the cultivation of an interest in the other person. In view of the fact that the earth gets old and moves toward its destruction, the real question and task is: Who is the human being? What is the nature of the human being?

First, we must look at each human being we meet in a rich, threefold way without judging too early. We must learn to look at the child in a way that enables us to gain a transparent picture of her. We must get to know the child through her way of walking, the shape of her head, the position of her eyes—because all of this tells us something about her essential being. If we look at the human being and try to penetrate the outer, we come to the Creator. If someone is imitated, it is always the gestures that are imitated. Therefore we should always observe the child's gestures and in particular her way of walking. Are we able to recollect in the evening how the child places her foot on the ground? But these are only the coarsest characteristics. The finer details bring us close to the essential being of the child.

We live presently at the threshold between the world of the senses and the world of spirit. Rudolf Steiner said: "Humanity has crossed the threshold without being aware of it." The great danger at the threshold is that the ego loses mastery over thinking, feeling, and willing. These faculties of the soul separate from each other. In our everyday life this threshold is always very close and we meet it constantly. If, for instance, I hold a glass of water in my hand and place it on the table, and I am conscious of my gesture, then I bring something over from the spiritual world. The work of the consciousness soul must be performed in full presence of mind and manifest outwardly. How do I peel an apple most skillfully? How do I arrange my domestic work most efficiently? Here thought is united with the will and the smallest deed becomes an ideal. To these daily situations belong, of course, celebrations of festivals. If, for example, we carry the dead in our consciousness, if we celebrate a festival of a particular kind when a grandmother has died, then not only death and destruction is experienced, but also how we live on with someone after he or she has died.

If we constantly recognize the other human being as a child of God, if we treat everything with care and love, then we work in a way that will not let us fall prey to destruction. Where human beings are connected with each other in love, here we build temples in the realm of spirit where we will find each other again. It is the task of the consciousness soul to live in such thoughts again and again.

Bibliography:

Rudolf Steiner, *Festivals and Their Meaning.* "*The Whitsun Mystery and its connection with the Ascension*" Domach, May 7, 1923, (Rudolf Steiner Press, London, 1981).

Rudolf Steiner, *The Fall of the Spirits of Darkness.* Lectures 4 and 5, Domach, October 6-7, 1917, (Rudolf Steiner Press, Bristol, England, 1993).

Dr. von Kügelgen spent thirty years as a teacher at the original Waldorf school in Stuttgart, and was the founder of the International Association of Waldorf Kindergartens. The article above was taken from notes by Sandra Czemnel-Sodergren at the International Kindergarten Conference in September 1995 and reprinted with permission from the International Waldorf Kindergarten Association.

The Religion of the Young Child

Elisabeth Moore-Haas

I once asked some American students of my course on early childhood education, what earliest memories they had of childhood. One student reported having seen a dog that he was not supposed to see, lying dead under an outside staircase. Later the dog was gone. The child crept under the staircase, then lay down and imitated the dog in death. He felt, "Oh, this is good." He was about three years old. It felt natural to him to experience the gesture of the dog.

I will give you an example of a child not being able to join others in imitation. At one time in Switzerland there were many Italian construction workers, and some children in my kindergarten would imitate them in play. A new child entered the kindergarten, and after a time came to me in tears: "I can't play with the other children! I don't understand what they are saying. They speak Italian!" On another occasion a boy brought an apple for his snack, but did not eat it. Instead he was spinning it slowly around staring at it. At last I asked him, "Will you eat your apple now?" He looked anxiously at me and said, "I can't. It has vitamins inside it." The child in the first example lived in the religion of the young child, but not the other two. It was the first who lived deeply into imitation, into the being of another.

Speaking about the incarnating ego of the child, Rudolf Steiner described the process in this way:

Out of the spiritual worlds—on spiritual wings, as it were—there comes the human ego. Observing first the child in the early years of life—how the child develops, how step by step the physiognomy emerges from inner depths to the surface of the body, how the child acquires more and more control over the physical organism—we see in this process, essentially, the incorporation of the ego. . . .The organizing principle in the physical body emerges with the change of teeth, becomes emancipated at this time, and in the main constitutes the intelligence. (*Balance in Teaching*, Sept. 22, 1920)

We hear a lot about the "dreamy" child. What does this mean? It is not that the child is daydreaming; rather it is a state of consciousness like that of adults when they are dreaming during sleep. The child's astral forces and ego are expanded. The ego is "observing the child." It is not yet incarnated or incorporated into the body. When very young children draw, they are sometimes amazed to see lines on the paper. They do not connect their movement with what is appearing on the paper. Only gradually do children connect actions with outcomes.

A very small baby looks at us, but looks above us. It does not make eye contact with us at first. The infant gives itself up to the atmosphere around it. We experience this, for example, in the lovely special aroma of a young baby. If we don't rush the baby down to earth, then it can live in this atmosphere and gradually enter the more earthly realm.

Then comes a stage around age three when the child says, "No, I don't want to." She has discovered something new, the possibility for "antipathy." In general, the child until age seven lives in the forces of sympathy and is at one with the world. But at times antipathy enters, though in a non-moral way. It is a way of standing back and looking at the world around one, similar to what happens later in life in reflective thinking.

True motivation arises out of sympathy. For a grown-up person, it may be a duty we have chosen or an inner commitment. The moment you expect the child to do something for you, however, he may rebel and misbehave. From this we can learn how to meet the child's true needs. There should be no expectations in regard to young children. An example of this would be a teacher who prepared a festival and did everything very well, but the children acted up and did not behave the way she wanted them to, because they felt pressed by her expectations. What is needed is a non-intentional approach towards the child.

This is also true for working with our colleagues, for example, regarding how they paint with their children or whether or not they use plant dyes. It is best not to have such expectations. Let them be. Then one can work freely with the other. We need to be in a state of sympathy with the children or with our colleagues. Then we can create something in the social realm. There is never only "one way." There are as many ways as there are kindergarten teachers! We cannot copy one another. We can digest what we see and hear and then come to our own way, which may turn out quite similar, but we have worked it through ourselves. Rudolf Steiner visited a school with parallel classes where the two teachers did things very differently. That's how it should be, he said. Each one must do it differently.

To decide what is right, you have to look at your particular situation. With young children you cannot try many different ways to do something. Out of intuition you must choose one that you think will fit this situation. For example, there was a kindergarten in Switzerland where all the children arrived by school bus at the same time. On the bus were older children, and when the kindergarten children entered their kindergarten room they were unable to play or imitate at first. They were too agitated. The teacher therefore decided to begin each day with a little table play. The children would enter a darkened room, a candle was lit, and the little play was performed. It worked for this class. It takes a true intuition to find the right solution to such a problem. Not just anything will do.

For the child, being able to play requires being in a state of sympathy. As adults we stand back from a beautiful sight and admire it. But the child has to enter right in and touch the thing. A third grader went to the mountains with her parents. They raved about the far-off snowy peaks, but she was only interested in seeing the flowers, the bees, and the stones—the things nearby, which she could embrace. She didn't even see the mountains. In adults, however, if this force of sympathy becomes too great it can be a problem.

Being in sympathy means being able to take in everything that is moving and that has a gesture. This is the realm where imitation lives. It matters what living images are rendered to the children. When we do a harvest circle with the children, for example, we often try to show the child what the farmer actually does. Is this really what the child needs? Is this not a "hidden teaching," especially if you go out and look at the farmers doing it and try to duplicate their gestures. This is a materialistic approach. We should look instead to the inner gesture of the activity. What really lives in the process? For example, in milling there is the archetypal gesture of two surfaces grinding against each other, which we can show by the palms moving round and round each other in a mill-like gesture without touching. This is similar to the eurythmy gesture for "M," which is the inner essence of the gesture. In this way we do not make the gestures too physical, such as would occur if we would show a turning handle of a hand mill. Children live in the inner gesture. We do not want to force their egos. We would like to create the right conditions for them to incorporate themselves.

The word "religion" comes from the Latin, "religio," which means to re-connect. Rudolf Steiner says the religious mood of the young child is experienced in a bodily, physical way, unlike the religious experience of an adult. All that lives in the child's environment influences the child's circulation, breathing, et cetera. The child is at one with the world, giving itself over to its environment, and that is the "religion of the child." Therefore, we need to prepare the environment so that children are able to give themselves up to it. All that we think or feel or do affects them. If all of this is done in a healthy way, then the young child does not need "religion" per se. The child is already there in religion.

But, of course, as the child becomes more distant from the environment, and rhythm becomes necessary to enable the child to "live into" the environment. Where there is life, there is rhythm. Rhythm serves as a bridge between the heavenly and the physical. For the child, rhythm in life can lead toward a healthy dream consciousness, which expresses itself often in liveliness (not hyperactivity), in creative play rather than in a dull brooding.

What about music in the mood of the fifth? It is different from what is called pentatonic music. Some people mistakenly think it is a "spaced out" music. Rudolf Steiner describes it very clearly. It is a type of music that helps a child to incarnate gently. With such music (as well as inner gestures, a healthy environment, and a sound rhythm), we create an oasis for children where they feel at home, and which will help them "love to incarnate." Such an experience serves as a healthy, homeopathic dose to balance some of the awakening influences of our time. If doing curative eurythmy for only three minutes a day can bring about healing in an adult, imagine the strengthening and healing that can occur in a healthy kindergarten day of four hours.

Rudolf Steiner also said that children should enjoy life and take pleasure in it. This is not the time to be ascetic. How can a young child who possesses nothing, not even love, become a giving person in adulthood? A natural egotism is appropriate in childhood.

When we intellectualize and give explanations, we cut off the child's "religion." The child is awakened prematurely and is perhaps afraid, such as the little boy with the apple who could not eat it because he was thinking of the vitamins it contained. The situation was similar for the little boy who could not play with his classmates for he thought they were speaking Italian. The child could not "dive in."

As teachers we must be careful not to use the children as a substitute for something we are missing; we should not want their love. We should be happiest when the children are completely absorbed in their play. Then they are deeply content. In imitation, the child takes in the quality of everything we do. She absorbs our ambitions, our intentions, and our quiet enthusiasm. Rudolf Steiner says we should be "actively thinking" when we are with children, because this allows them to be in a dream consciousness. The more we as adults achieve wakeful consciousness, the more the children can have a dream consciousness.

All of this calls for selflessness on the part of the adult. In addition to an appropriate atmosphere in the early childhood room and in our carrying of ourselves, the "religion of the young child" can also be helped by the clothing we wear. The image that humanity was once in paradise is related to the "religion of the young child." It means being united with the spiritual world, being at one. After eating the apple, we human beings entered a much more materialistic state of consciousness. We could no longer see the human being veiled in the colors of the astral body. But the child still feels at home with clothes that are a picture of the spiritual, rather than pants or jeans which point to the physical, namely to the form of the skeleton. There are teachers who may wear jeans or pants out on the street and then change to more appropriate clothes for the early childhood surroundings. We need to dress in such a way that the child feels comfortable and "at home" with our clothing.

We affect the children in so many ways. Our morality and our thoughts permeate even the child's sheaths. Rudolf Steiner said that children could behave like little demons. How are we to handle these demons? By behaving in an appropriate way in the child's environment. Steiner said that we should make the same impression on the child as her own arm makes. We should be like an extension of her own body. Then we are not imposing ourselves on her or forcing something. "Education throughout life is self-education." In a lecture on the self-education of the human being in the light of spiritual science, given in Berlin on March 14, 1912 and not yet published in English, Rudolf Steiner said the following:

If we speak of an extended self in each of us through which we can enter into other individualities—in sympathy or in sharing joy, for example—then, with the developing child we can speak of something else that is present beyond our usual considerations, something that develops out of the ordinary consciousness. This is the presence of a higher being present outside the child's usual self and already at work on the child. Where can we free what is already actively working on the child as a higher self, as a higher entity belonging to the child but not entering the child's consciousness? It may seem peculiar but it is nevertheless correct that the entity is active in the child during rational, well-guided play.

We can only create an environment that facilitates the play of the child. What is actually achieved through play is essentially accomplished through the self-initiated activity of the child, through everything that cannot be regulated by us through strict rules. Indeed, this is the essential aspect, the educational aspect of play—which we cease with our rules, with our pedagogical artistry and educational techniques, and give the child over to his or her own forces. For what does the child do when we give him over to his own forces? The child then explores, by playing with physical objects, whether this or that works through his own activity. He brings his own will into activity, into movement. And through the manner in which these physical objects behave under the influence of his will, it comes about that the child educates himself through life itself, even if this takes place playfully in a completely different manner than through the influence of a personality or a pedagogical principle.

It is therefore of the greatest importance that we interfere as little as possible in the play of the child. Thus if we give the child a toy with which he can, through pulling strings or in some other way, receive the illusion of the movements of the human beings or of objects, whether through a movable picture book or some other toy, we educate the child better through such play than if we were to give him building blocks. Too much rational activity is intermingled, and this belongs to a more personal principle than the playful tapping around with the living, moving element that is not grasped conceptually but is simply observed in its full activity. The less thought-through and predetermined this is, which a game or toy reveals, the better; because it then becomes possible for something higher, which cannot be forced into human consciousness, to enter, because the child is exploring and is not relating to life in a rational, intellectual way. And then we can see how the child is already being educated by something that transcends the personal.

The higher self of the child can come in if we can provide the appropriate environment. This is education toward freedom. Then, within the morning, we can offer a little ritual in a homeopathic dose, such as a verse of Rudolf Steiner's. These special moments might create an atmosphere into which the hierarchies may be experienced.

Questions and Answers

Q: Could you say more about religion in our time and in the future? Also, is it still appropriate to do a shepherd's play with the children? Is it right to have the Sistine Madonna *in the kindergarten?*

A: Sometimes we find ourselves doing things in the kindergarten that seem very religious, and we must realize that we are doing these things for ourselves, as adults. We are reminding ourselves of the background of the festivals and their religious content. At such times we are not doing things with the children's needs in mind.

Between ages seven and fourteen children live in the world of feeling and "religion" is more appropriate to them. But the first seven years are a time of doing. Sometimes our kindergartens appear overly Christian in a sectarian way. We also must consider what lives in the culture where the school is located.

Rudolf Steiner has said that in the future we will be connected to the spiritual world, but, unlike the child, we will be connected consciously. Then we will not feel the need for *re-ligio*, for reconnecting, for we will already be connected. We haven't reached this stage yet, however. Young people are sensitive to the "exclusive" aspect of religion and wish to open to all. Rudolf Steiner has said that each religion is an aspect of the whole.

When we study religion more deeply we can see that true Christianity is not restricted to one place or one people, and it is, in its essence, a non-denominational and all-inclusive religion. The Christ being is of a cosmic, universal nature. When we have this in mind we can say that Christianity has a central place in Waldorf education, but not in a narrow sectarian sense. We don't yet have true freedom of religion, though younger people are straining towards this.

Regarding the Sistine Madonna, we must realize that we do not hang this painting in the kindergarten for religious reasons. We should study what Rudolf Steiner has said about Raphael and about this painting.
We need to understand what it says about incarnation, about the soul carrying the spirit into incarnation. It is important, however, that we treat the painting with modesty. It should not give the impression of an altar or a shrine. It does not need to be draped with cloth. Its presence should not be exaggerated, and it should not carry a quality of sentimentality. This would be as inappropriate as saying a verse sentimentally with young children.

When we say a verse or a prayer with the children, we might not use gestures. As much as we otherwise try to include movement whenever we can; the verse works in a different realm. We should look cheerfully at the children while saying the verse. Our eyes should not be closed in a mood of inwardness. That is not appropriate with young children. If one finds that the snack verse becomes too routine for the children, one may occasionally speak a verse by Rudolf Steiner which is generally more appropriate for adults.

In preparing for a festival, study a lecture on that festival very carefully. When you are carrying the festival inwardly, you do not have to do so much outwardly with the children. For example, at Michaelmas time, I like to do a modest marionette play of St. George and the dragon, which includes Michael. I find Michaelmas an inwardly richer festival than Christmas. It is our inner work that prepares this. If it lives in the teacher, the festival may become more elaborate. It will not hurt the children as long as you do not explain.

Q: Could you say more about active thinking?

A: We must learn to observe how imitation works and lives in the quality of movement. When the teacher acts, the child takes in the quality, the morality of how the person moves. It does not necessarily happen that the children do the same thing that the teacher does, but rather that the quality of the teacher's activity is brought by the children into what they do. The quality of our thinking and striving towards the spiritual will express itself in the finest ways of our demeanor.

For the adult, being Michaelic means being conscious, being awake. But for the young child, awakeness is not appropriate. For children to grow properly into awakeness, they must first sleep properly. But children benefit from our awakeness. Rudolf Steiner has said that if we work, usually with his book, *How to Know Higher Worlds,* for instance, that is a life force for the children.

The child's etheric realm is attacked by the media. Since Waldorf education keeps children open and therefore "soft," they are more damaged by the media than children who are not in Waldorf schools. We take on a heavy karma if we don't get our courage up to take a stand on television. But we must not do this out of dogmatism. We have to do our homework and study the effects of television on children. There are many books on this subject by non-anthroposophic authors. We ought to study them in order to include scientific research in our arguments.

Q: Is discipline too awakening?

A: It all depends upon how it is done. We must act on the children's behalf. When children act up, they may not be "tuning their instruments" (the physical body) in a healthy way. Children are often already damaged and they need healing. We accomplish this, however, through deeds rather than through words. We do not need to say, "This little dwarf needs to go to bed now" at clean-up time. We hand the child a log to put away, but don't watch to be sure that he does it, for that would be too intentional. The word "clean-up" is taboo. It is so abused at home that it has a bad connotation for the children.

Q: Could you say more about the mood of the fifth?

A: Fortunately, more music in the mood of the fifth is becoming available. A Swiss woman, Helga Oberlander, has helped to create four seasonal books of mood of the fifth songs. Young children do not need the personal, more inward soul mood of minor or major music. Mood of the fifth music strives to live in the middle. It does not just go up and down the pentatonic scale. It always "dissolves" into the fifth.

Elisabeth Moore-Haas was a kindergarten teacher in Switzerland and is the founder and director of the kindergarten training seminar in Berne, Switzerland. She taught in early childhood education programs in North America as a visiting faculty member for many years.

*The Gateway of Birth
– the Sistine Madonna*

Raphael's Sistine Madonna: Is It Appropriate in the Kindergarten?

René Querido

Of the countless masterpieces of Renaissance painting, perhaps none occupies such a remarkable position as the *Sistine Madonna* by Raphael. It embodies in a superb manner great contrasts: the painting is both magnificent and intimate in character, heavenly and earthly in mood, sacred and secular in portraying the mysteries of motherhood and the eternal feminine.

Raphael (1483-1520), who was born on one Good Friday and died on another at the early age of thirty–seven, is said to have painted the *Sistine Madonna* at thirty-four or thirty-five. It therefore belongs to the artist's later period. Although it served as an altarpiece for a number of years, the original intention for it may have been a very different one. Executed on canvas rather than on a wooden panel as was the custom, it may have been painted expressly to be carried in processions through the crowded streets of Rome at high festivals of the Virgin Mary. This would also suggest that it was meant, in spite of its magnificence and considerable size, to be a work of art for the people at large and not simply for the clergy or nobility.

For the past two hundred and fifty years or so it has hung in the National Gallery in Dresden, Germany, a once beautiful city struck by a bombing raid at the end of the Second World War. The painting survived the many vicissitudes of wars, revolutions and insurrections from the eighteenth century onward. Among its admirers are such various and distinguished personalities as Goethe, Novalis, and Dostoyevski.

Today one approaches the original canvas, measuring some eight or nine feet in height—the figures are life size—from the end of a long gallery. The experience as one slowly moves toward the Madonna is indeed truly overwhelming, for as one draws near, one senses that the central figure carrying the child gently strides toward the beholder like some supersensible revelation. With the green curtains on either side drawn, we seem to cross a threshold into a heavenly realm, where against a background of number-less angelic faces and supported by billowing clouds, the mystery of motherhood and of Mary with the child is revealed. The central female figure combines a serene, divine countenance with great earthly beauty. Raphael may well have been inspired by one of his many beautiful models, but here he transformed the experience into a heavenly countenance. The child is remarkably awake and knowing for one so young, as if he were aware of the thorny road that he is destined to tread on the earth.

Too little attention has been given to the two saints that flank the central figure. They form an intrinsic part of the composition, as indeed do the two winged cherubic beings at the foot of the painting who peek at the events above with a quiet, somewhat mischievous, childlike curiosity. Saint Sixtus II, a magnificent old man clad in golden papal robes, is seen at left, looking up in deep reverence and conscious recognition at the mother and child. His right arm and hand point outward to the beholder while his left hand rests with a warm, sympathetic gesture on his heart.

In strong contrast we have on our right a portrayal of the young, beautiful Saint Barbara whose head is turned with lowered gaze towards us, her hands folded in devotion across her breast. The historical background of these two figures will give further meaning to the total composition. Both Saint Barbara (235-313) and Sixtus II (pope: 257-258) lived in Italy during the third century A.D., when the original Christ impulse in its fullness had not yet been impeded by church dogma and state approval.

Barbara, renowned for her beauty, was locked up in a tower by her father, who feared that she had become a Christian. She maintained her faith and suffered horrible torture, which left her disfigured for life. Her father ordered her killed, but legend has it that, as the execution was to be accomplished, he was struck by lightning. Saint Barbara lived into her late seventies and was known for her loving, caring deeds for the poor and ailing.

Sixtus II, who only occupied the papal chair for one year, was able at a time of terrible conflict to bring about peace. He did so by renouncing power. Widely admired for his magnanimity and benevolence, he was canonized shortly after his death and was regarded with special veneration, together with Saint Laurentius, by many generations right up to the Renaissance. These two biographical vignettes will help us to understand Raphael's wise choice in portraying just these particular saints on either side of Mary and the Child. They represent archetypes: Sixtus of power transformed into peace, Barbara of the sacrifice of beauty to spiritual love, both inspired by the eternal feminine that had borne the child. Indeed, if we then view the central figure also as a divine archetype made manifest on earth in all her glory, beauty, and inner serene strength, this masterpiece is lifted out of a one–sided, dogmatic interpretation. It is not merely a Christian painting in the narrow sense of the word. It can appeal strongly and intimately to men and women of any religious persuasion—Christians, Hebrews, Buddhists alike—if it is seen as representing an ideal of conscious, yet eternal, motherhood carrying the child, awakening from innocence to strong deeds of love. Such representations are also found in other cultures: in Isis and the child Horus, in Kwan Yin, or the Canon of the Orient.

Let us now deal with the question: Should a reproduction of the *Sistine Madonna* necessarily be displayed in our kindergartens, and if so, why?

In 1911 Rudolf Steiner gave indications to Dr. Peipers in Munich that a healing influence proceeds from contemplating again and again a series of Raphael's Madonnas in reproduction arranged in the form of a Pentagram. The series of fifteen pictures, mostly Madonnas by Raphael (there is one by Donatello and one by Michelangelo), opens with the *Sistine Madonna*, whose composition itself is clearly based on the pentagram, and culminates in Raphael's Transfiguration, his last, unfinished painting. Astonishingly, powerful healing can be obtained even by meditating upon these pictures in black and white reproductions, as was the case in Steiner's time when he gave the indication to Dr. Peipers for his patients.

How are we to understand this process? In our circles we are familiar with the soul strengthening that can be received by meditating regularly on a verse or mantra. Such words—and Rudolf Steiner has provided us with hundreds of verses for particular occasions—contain through their meaning, sound, cadence, and composition a power to awaken new faculties in the soul. For the teacher this is of special significance, for such inner activity, regularly practiced in the stillness of the soul, makes us more able to cope with the task of caring for and educating children.

What is perhaps less familiar is the use of the Yantra, as it is known in the East: a picture, a scroll of calligraphy (practiced in particular by the Japanese), or a statue, which through its mere presence in a hall, a place of worship, or a private room endows the space with an uplifting mood. Without using this terminology, Rudolf Steiner practiced the use of signs and symbols in a similar manner for the first time at the Munich Conference of 1907. There he directed that the walls of the hall where the Rosicrucian Conference was to take place be draped from top to floor with curtains of bright vermilion. It was also on this occasion that the occult signs and seals were first displayed together with models of the pillars of Joachim and Boaz from the Temple of Solomon. Rudolf Steiner pointed out that only under these conditions could certain supersensible beings participate in the earthly happening. He also indicated that occult teachings should never again be severed from the artistic impulse.

Later, in 1913–14, in the whole complex construction of the first Goetheanum and its arrangements of inner and outer spaces, pillars with carved capitals, engraved colored windows, and painted cupolas, the same theme appears in a more comprehensive and powerful way. Space, color, and form can exert a direct, beneficent healing influence and, under certain circumstances, are able to awaken dominant spiritual powers in the beholder. In the light of the above, we need to tread a balanced path between sentimentality and cold abstraction in determining the role of the *Sistine Madonna* in the kindergarten. To exclude this masterpiece altogether seems foolish. If parents object to its presence on religious grounds, we should attempt to educate them to a wider viewpoint. Each kindergarten teacher has to use her or his tact and discretion. What matters is that one has oneself come to an inner conviction over a period of time and speaks to the hearts and minds of the parents out of a depth of personal experience.

Equally, it is inappropriate to build an altar draped with colored veils around the *Sistine Madonna*. A shrine-like display with candles will justifiably create uneasiness in many parents, even among those who are genuinely interested in the new mysteries revealed through anthroposophy. Our task therefore is a difficult one: to learn to appreciate that this superb masterpiece combines a serene, sober mood with divine revelation and is utterly devoid of sentimentality. Can we therefore accord the *Sistine Madonna* a special place in the room in a simple, straightforward manner, bearing in mind that the children's attention need not be drawn to it? It acts in a healing, peaceful manner through its very presence.

A final word: it may be helpful to consider whether it would not be preferable to display the full reproduction in a large print (considering the size of the original) rather than making do with a detail of the painting. This is especially so because the flanking figures express through gesture and mood the qualities of peace and love. The cherubic figures at the foot of the painting contribute a delightful quality of childlike innocence.

René Querido was the director and founder of Rudolf Steiner College in Fair Oaks, CA and lectured on Waldorf education and anthroposophy internationally. He is now retired. This article is a revised version of a talk to Waldorf kindergarten teachers during the Western Regional Teachers Conference in February, 1989, held at Rudolf Steiner College in Fair Oaks, California.

The Sistine Madonna in the Waldorf Kindergarten: Working with the Imagination

Joan Almon

Raphael's *Sistine Madonna* is often found in Waldorf kindergartens, but unfortunately many misunderstandings have arisen about its presence in recent years. The most common is that it is viewed as part of a religious shrine with Mary and her child worshiped as they might be in a church setting. Kindergarten teachers sometimes contribute to this misunderstanding by draping the painting with cloth. When it is hung over the nature table in this way, it does give the impression of an altar.

The *Sistine Madonna's* presence in a kindergarten is a quiet one. It may hang over the nature table or at another place, but it is not the focus of worship or even of attention. Rather it is a quiet reminder of the great journey that every human soul makes from the heavenly world to the earthly. Here the child is at the threshold of birth, an open door to the earthly world. The child does not come alone into the world. It is accompanied by the mother. In physical birth we are aware of the mother's great role in bringing her child through the portal of birth. Here, the artist is showing another aspect of the experience—the mother helping usher her child into birth at a spiritual level. Her billowing veil and her protecting arms surround the child. Her whole being embraces him and carries him across the threshold. The painting is a spiritual counterpart to the physical experience of embracing the child in the womb and bringing it forth into the physical world. One could say it is the other half of the pregnancy and birth process, which is a profoundly physical experience. What lifts the experience and makes it physically bearable for the mother—and also for the child—is the spiritual dimension that rays through it.

What is the purpose of placing this particular painting in a kindergarten? As far as I know, Rudolf Steiner did not speak of this painting with Elisabeth Grunelius, the first Waldorf kindergarten teacher. His indications about its use were given, in part, in the context of advice to pregnant mothers. He suggested that they meditate on the picture. Looking at it from the mother's perspective, one can feel the strength of the picture, the quiet power of a mother guiding her child to the earth. How is it for the child to have this picture hanging quietly in the room?

Although I lived with the painting in my kindergarten for many years, I never spoke with the children about it. It hung as a quiet reminder of a profound experience that they had recently had. They never spoke to me about it, either, except on one occasion. Young Daniel, age four, was gazing and gazing at the painting. I hovered nearby, wondering if he would have anything to say about it. At last he awoke from his reverie, gave himself a little shake, turned and saw me standing there and said, "She has really big feet doesn't she?" It seemed like such a mundane remark after the reverent way he had gazed at it. Later, I wondered if this remark alluded to Mary's ability to stand upon her feet, albeit on the clouds, and to bring her child into incarnation. In other paintings of Mary and her child she is shown sitting. It is unusual to see her standing in her full uprightness. In fact, at the moment, I can think of no other example of her standing and holding her baby. I will never be quite sure what Daniel meant, but in general I felt the children took comfort from having this picture in their environment. It was such a quiet reminder of their own journey to earth, not so long ago, and of the loving arms that guided them. They did not make the great journey alone. Especially for children who faced trauma and serious difficulties on the earth, the presence of this picture seemed to be a great help.

The questions most frequently asked regarding the *Sistine Madonna* are why it is necessary to have a Christian portrayal of the mother and child. Could it not be a more archetypal pair, less identified with the Christian church? The other question is why it needs to be a Caucasian mother and child. Could it not be a mother and child of color? In living with these questions, I found two different ways to approach them. The first was to realize that this particular painting is quite different from other Madonna paintings, even others by Raphael. I would not normally want to hang a Madonna painting in a Waldorf kindergarten, for it is an image closely associated with one religion, and most often with one race. I would find this inappropriate for a Waldorf kindergarten, which usually serves families of many religions and many races. This painting has a special quality, however, in the way it portrays the mother and child in the spiritual world with the faces of many other beings looking on, partially hidden in the clouds. They seem to be other souls, waiting for their turn to incarnate. This particular painting is so profound and so universal that its effect seems to offset the concerns about its religious or racial associations. In my own kindergarten, questions frequently arose about it from the parents, or from colleagues, questions which often led me to go deeper into my own understanding of the painting. It is never good for such an image to be around and simply become a habit. After conversations with the parents, for instance, a deeper understanding developed, and it was possible to continue to benefit from the presence of the image in the kindergarten. For some parents and teachers, however, this is not the case, and their concerns are strong enough that it is not possible to have the *Sistine Madonna* itself in the kindergarten. Unfortunately, the whole image of bringing the child to earth from the heavenly world may then be lost to the children. Is there an alternative?

I continue to feel that the image itself is much needed by the children, perhaps even more so today than in recent decades, for the attack on childhood grows ever stronger and the child's need for protection is greater than before. The image of coming to earth surrounded by the mother's being is an ultimate image of safety and protection for the child. Is there an alternative to the *Sistine Madonna* that would have spiritual integrity and meet the needs of the children?

Considering these questions brought me to a new approach. In working with Rudolf Steiner's lectures, *The Four Seasons and the Archangels* (Rudolf Steiner Press, 1984), I was struck by the imagination that Rudolf Steiner perceived in the spiritual world for the winter season, which is remarkably similar to what

Raphael captured in the Sistine Madonna. Rudolf Steiner describes the winter imagination in terms of a mother and child of profoundly cosmic nature with a deep relationship to the Sun, the Moon, and the stars. They are not an earthly pair in the usual sense, but are in fact so cosmic and universal that they can transcend earthly experiences of religion or race. Rudolf Steiner describes their nature in this way:

> The head of Mary is like a radiant star, which means that her whole countenance and bearing must give expression to this star-radiant quality. If then we turn to the breast, we come to the breathing process: to the Sun-element, the child, forming itself out of the clouds in the atmosphere, shot through by the rays of the sun. . . Beneath the mother's feet and around her in the clouds are the forces of the Moon and Earth, and the clouds are filled with many human heads, pressing downward.

One element of the imagination is however different from Raphael's painting. Raphael portrayed the threshold between heavenly and earthly worlds with an open green curtain. The angle is such that one looks up from the earth and beholds the mother and child standing in the opening of the curtain. Rudolf Steiner, on the other hand, describes the imagination as if looking down to earth from the Cosmos. Speaking of the full imagination, he says, "All of this would really have to be shown through a kind of rainbow coloring. For if we were to look down from the cosmos toward the Earth, through the shining of the stars, it would be as though the Earth were wishing to shine inwardly, beneath its surface, in rainbow colors."

The whole of the winter imagination is a beautiful picture of birth, including the rainbow. For the young child the rainbow is often associated with birth. One child, while looking at a rainbow in the sky, said, "Oh look Mommy, a rainbow. A child's being born." Another child lived in a dry part of Spain but knew rainbows from his summers in Germany. One day he asked his mother, "Mommy, how are babies born in Spain? There are no rainbows here." In my collection of children's drawings there is one of a rainbow with a child sitting upon it and sliding down to earth. Another is by a six-year-old who was attending her sibling's birth. Prominent in her picture is a rainbow.

How was Raphael able to capture this imagination of cosmic birth, albeit from an earthly vantage point? Rudolf Steiner speaks of this when he says that the winter imagination of mother and child "hovered so often before painters in earlier times, especially in the first Christian centuries" and that "the after effects have been preserved in Raphael's *Sistine Madonna*."

Perhaps it is time for Waldorf kindergarten teachers to live so deeply into the winter imagination of mother and child that they find their own way to portray the imagination through paint, crayon, or even wool pictures. It can then portray the essential journey of mother and child from the spiritual to the earthly world in a way that is not so associated with a particular religion, race, or culture. Such a portrayal might hang only in the winter season, or throughout the year as a reminder of the great moment of birth and the loving protection that guards each child who comes to the earth. The effort made by the teacher to penetrate this mighty imagination will be a great gift to the children, even if the artistry is not on a level with Raphael.

Joan Almon is co-founder of the Waldorf Early Childhood Association of North America, the General Secretary of the Anthroposophical Society, and is the U.S. Coordinator of the Alliance for Childhood.

The Sistine Madonna: "A Symbol of the Eternal Spirituality in People"

Dr. Helmut von Kügelgen

Why did Rudolf Steiner advise mothers-to-be to look often at Raphael's painting? He mentions it in many contexts, and some of these comments help one to understand this advice. Those who try, while contemplating this painting, to describe and express in words what they are seeing, feeling, and understanding, will surely find the answer. With this in mind, the following quotations from lectures are meant to deepen and make conscious that experience.

Rudolf Steiner, in a lecture given January 30, 1913:

> Let us now allow one of Raphael's paintings to make an impression upon us. It is the *Sistine Madonna,* which is located in Dresden and which probably each one of us knows from the numerous copies that have been spread throughout the world. It stands before us as one of the most splendid, most noble artworks of human development. The mother appears to us with the child, floating on the air, down from the clouds that surround the earth, floating out of the undefined, one might even say out of the spiritual, super-sensible world. She is clothed and surrounded by clouds, which, as if of their own accord, become similar to human forms.
>
> One of the clouds, as if solidified, resembles the child of the Madonna. As she appears there, she brings forth in us quite special feelings about which we might well say that, when these feelings pass through our soul, we could forget all the legendary ideas out of which the picture of the Madonna has grown, and we could forget all Christian traditions which tell us about the Madonna. I would like to put forward this opinion about what we can experience in the presence of this Madonna—not to characterize it in a dry manner but rather to characterize it in the most heartfelt way possible. Whoever considers the development of humankind from the point of view of spiritual science comes to the conclusion that the human being existed before the beings of the animal, plant, and even mineral realms existed. The painting of the Madonna with the child is the symbol of the eternal spirituality in people, which certainly comes to the earth from beyond. Yet, this painting, through parted clouds, has everything that can only arise or proceed from the earthly.

Rudolf Steiner, in a lecture given December 22, 1908:

> And Raphael has, in a wonderfully delicate and pure way, revealed this mystery by showing how, out of the spiritual heads of the little angels, the Madonna, the human being, takes shape and brings forth anew the blossom of Jesus of Nazareth, who is to receive the Christ-seed. The entire evolution of humankind is wonderfully contained in this painting of the Madonna!

Rudolf Steiner in a lecture given July 6, 1915: (*Destinies of Individualities and Nations,* Rudolf Steiner Press, London, 1986.)

> One can see in the *Sistine Madonna* that a great cosmic mystery is being impressed upon human hearts, and one will be able to build upon this in the future. When humanity will have come to the type of non-denominational, broad and encompassing Christianity that spiritual science already represents today, one will be able to continue building up this wonderful mystery that has influenced human minds just as the *Sistine Madonna* has done. Often it has been proven to me that when you look into the eyes of children, you can know that something looks out from the children's eyes that did not enter their being during birth, something that shines out of the depths of human souls. If one looks at the children in Raphael's Madonna paintings, one sees the same elements of that which is divine, secret, and beyond the human in their eyes as are still in the eyes of a child shortly after birth. One can observe this in all Raphael's paintings of children with one single exception. One of the children in his paintings cannot be interpreted in this way, and it is the Baby Jesus of the *Sistine Madonna.* Upon looking into the eyes of this child, one realizes that there is already more to him than is possible in a human being. Raphael has made the difference that, in this single child of the *Sistine Madonna,* something is living that from the outset is experienced as purely spiritual and Christ-like.
>
> Since we are people with feelings, we are also creatures, beings of the hierarchies, and we also operate where the hierarchies operate. We work in this weaving, we perform deeds which are not for us alone but rather, through which we work together, on the entire structure of the world. Through our feelings we serve the higher beings whom are shaping the world. And if we believe, while viewing the *Sistine Madonna,* that we are gratifying the feeling that arises in us, it is a fact that a real process, a real event is taking place. If such feelings were not present, those beings who are supposed to be working on the structure of future conditions and incarnations on earth would not have the strength that they need for their work. Our feelings are as necessary for the structure of the houses that the gods are building in the world as are bricks for the construction of a person's house. And what we know about our feelings is once again only a part. We know what a joy it is to stand before the *Sistine Madonna.* But what happens there is a part of the whole world, and it is quite immaterial how we consciously approach it.

Rudolf Steiner in a lecture given January 17, 1915: (*Destinies of Individualities and Nations,* Rudolf Steiner Press, London, 1986.)

> And if you look at the wonderful painting called the *Mater Gloriosa,* who is receiving Faust's soul, there you have the counterpart to that to which Raphael alludes in his most famous painting, the *Sistine Madonna,* where the Virgin Mother is bringing the soul down here; at the end of *Faust,* we see how the Virgin Mother bears the soul upward—it is the soul's birth upon death.

Rudolf Steiner, in a lecture given Dresden, August 16, 1918:

> Thus I had always gazed in amazement upon the holy *Sistine Madonna* by Raphael, which I already knew earlier from copper engravings and copies, due to the world-encompassing look of the child and the deeply felt virginal countenance and being of the mother of this divine child. You see here represented with the world's greatest masterly strokes Child and God and Mother and Virgin all at the same time in divine radiance. This painting alone is a world, a very full artistic world, and it alone would have sufficed to make its creator immortal even if he had painted nothing else.

*The Gateway of Death
– Working with Death
in the Kindergarten*

After-Death Care at Home

Beth Knox

When death touches us deeply, it brings certainty with it. Every goodbye becomes sacred. Each exchange of love is precious. Every silence brings an opportunity to remember and listen to the love that connects us beyond this physical world. My seven-year-old daughter, Alison, passed from the earth suddenly in an auto accident in October of 1995. Death can happen that way.

When death comes, it is often expected; but all our partings from loved ones are painful, even unbearable. Our relationships change forever in that moment of a heartbeat, and we are left to adjust to this impossible, new reality.

Imagine facing the loss of a loved one. What happens? For an unexpected death, emergency services are called. Even if there are no signs of life, the individual will be taken to the hospital so that a doctor can pronounce death. The next destination is the hospital morgue until someone arrives from the funeral home. For an expected death at home or in a hospice facility, the funeral director is also called to take "the body" away.

How does the funeral home care for our dear one, whom we have loved for a lifetime? They come with their cart and vinyl body bag. They zip this precious vessel up and cart her away, put her in a refrigerated drawer, and make arrangements for us to "view" the body. They charge you for each aspect of service provided. This is on top of nearly $2,000 just to respond to your initial call as a "basic service fee." There are less expensive options, ones where you will never see your loved one again, because other people are now in control and you must conform to their schedule.

I was presented with all this at the time of my daughter's crossing. Until then the nine-year change had been my biggest concern for my children's welfare. I was totally unprepared, and my whole being recoiled from contemplating the next steps. Very few of us have visited the inner workings of a funeral home, but I knew that was not a place where I was sending my little girl.

My friends gathered around me at the hospital, some of whom had spent time with Nancy Poer. They informed me that I could take Alison home. My Christian Community priest arrived and helped me to navigate through other questions before me: autopsy, organ donation, and embalming. Once I was clear, it was as if the universe moved to fulfill my desires. I wanted my daughter's body disturbed as little as possible, and I brought her home for three days.

What I truly needed was reliable information on after-death care. There was no one to tell me that I could transport her myself and file all necessary paperwork. There was no information on how much dry ice to use so that she did not freeze solid. There was no one to tell me that the funeral home's insistence to "set her features" behind closed doors meant a wire in her jaw and caps under her eyelids, effects that could have been accomplished lovingly, in non–invasive ways. There was no guidance to tell me that handling all arrangements at home and opening my doors to family, friends, and neighbors would create a profound and unique experience of love and community. I was prey to what the funeral home told me in my numbed state. My truest and most reliable guide, as it turned out, was my love for Alison and her trust in me.

This experience was the inspiration behind CROSSINGS: Caring for Our Own at Death, a non-profit resource center that I co–founded with friends who supported me during Alison's crossing. We learned that in forty-four states the family can control the entire funeral process without employing a funeral director. We help families maintain their decision-making control and create an end of life that truly honors their loved one. We have gone into homes and guided families through the step-by-step, after-death care of their loved ones. We have also walked families through this process by telephone in conjunction with a resource guide that we sell, when they wanted to do everything themselves. We have offered workshops to communities who wish to become self–sufficient in this regard.

Word is spreading that the act of caring for our departed provides greater comfort and healing to families and communities. This is no longer a quiet practice in a local community. It has evolved into a healing journey, available to all who are asked to bear the unbearable. The response of families that we support affirms the sacred value of caring for our own after death.

For my part, I am grateful for anything that brings me closer to my daughter and the realms of spirit in which she dwells. Simultaneously, being able to bring some peace and comfort to families in the throes of grief is an experience of grace.

The full story of the crossing of Beth's daughter can be found in Alison's Gift *by Pat Hogan, available through the Anthroposophic Press. Beth Knox is the Executive Director and co-founder of CROSSINGS, Caring for Our Own at Death, a tax-exempt, educational organization dedicated to the renewal of simplicity and sanctity at the time of death. For more information contact Crossings,* P.O. Box 721, Silver Spring, MD 20918, 301–593-5451, email crossingcare@earthlink.net, Internet: www.crossings.net.

Helping Children in a Time of Trouble
Nancy Foster

In a time of trouble, such as the death of a family member or friend, parents are faced with the question of how to help the children through this time. In a sense, the question will have many as answers as there are particular children. Since children respond so differently to a situation, according to their age and nature. Parents are frequently brought up short by the realization that they must first face their own feelings and questions. Once these are addressed, it is possible to deal with the child's questions.

A generally-accepted "rule of thumb" in responding to children's questions is to give only as much information as the child is actually requesting. As adults, our thoughts on a topic tend to be quite far ranging, while the child's question is likely to be on a much more direct level. It is better to err on the side of simplicity; if a child needs to know more, another question will surely follow. Your answer to "what happens to someone who has died" will, of course, depend on your own view of this; in any case, a simple picture is usually best for a child. Your honest expression of sorrow and sympathy is very beneficial in helping a child to experience and cope with loss, but uncontrolled emotions are usually troubling or even frightening for the young child. The adult's efforts to recognize and accept grief without being overwhelmed by it can be a profound example to a child.

Some children may appear to become obsessed by the death, asking question after question and seeming unsatisfied by any number of answers. The sensitive parent will soon realize that this child is seeking for something other than words to quiet his or her anxieties. Often the best answer is a warm hug and words such as, "That's enough talk for now; come, it's time to pick some flowers for the supper table," (or some other such homely task). This child needs most of all an expression of love from the parent and the reassurance that life will go on, in the form of normal activities, even in the midst of grief. This is not to deny the grief, but to help the child work through it in the way most natural to children—through activity. If it seems appropriate, the child can be encouraged to help bake a loaf of bread for the bereaved family, or perhaps to make a card to send.

The place of ritual in helping children and adults to cope with loss should not be overlooked. Rituals are "special times for special happenings," in the words of Julius Segal, a psychologist writing in the *Washington Post* some years ago. Such rituals, which may be religious, secular, or familial in origin, "can provide a strengthening sense of order and meaning in times of trouble. They can help maintain the form and rhythm of lives shaken by trauma and grief. . . " Mr. Segal's theme was the role of ritual in creating a stable, fulfilling family life, but it can also be applied to times of trouble. For a child who shows a continuing, deep concern about a death, establishing a simple ritual can be very comforting. For example, the child may help to create a special setting with perhaps a candle, a small vase of flowers, some beautiful autumn leaves, some acorns or crystals. And at a particular time each day—just before or after dinner, possibly, or before the bedtime story—the candle may be lighted, a song sung, or a verse recited, "to send our thoughts" or "to send our love" to the one who has died or to that person's family. Such a ritual may serve as a kind of anchor in a sea of grief or anxiety, as well as diminishing the sense of helplessness in the face of another's loss.

Finally, a story that contains a simple but meaningful picture of the spiritual origin of life and its destinies can be of great help to a child. From such a story—as from all *true* stories—the child can take the image or images that will be of most help to him or her.

Nancy Foster has been a Waldorf early childhood educator since 1973 at Acorn Hill Waldorf Kindergarten and Nursery in Silver Spring, Maryland where she now works with parents and children in parent/child groups. She also lectures, offers workshops for Waldorf kindergarten teachers, and is on the visiting faculty of Sunbridge College in Spring Valley, New York. She is the author and editor of Let Us Form a Ring *and* Dancing as We Sing. *She and her husband, a professional musician, encountered Waldorf education and anthroposophy while seeking a school for their two sons, now grown.*

Helping Our Children and Loved Ones at the Threshold of Death

Nancy Jewel Poer

My mother, Lola Heckelman, an enthusiastic, longtime anthroposophist, died so quickly and unexpectedly that it took us all by surprise. But she picked a wonderfully propitious time for her transition into the spiritual world, February 27, 1979, the day of celebration of Rudolf Steiner's birthday in the one–hundreth Michaelic year. Little did I know that as she crossed over my threshold work would begin.

Though shattered and vulnerable with her sudden death, I accepted the destiny rightness of it all and knew that ultimately I would have perspective from the spiritual wisdom of Rudolf Steiner—a bigger and more universal context for my experience. What I wasn't prepared for was the amazing response to her passing of my mother's eleven grandchildren. I watched with wonder as it became evident that she had prepared them for her death by the way she had lived her life. It was such a vivid lesson in how our attitudes can nurture and sustain our loved ones left behind. Lola had an unquenchable enthusiasm for the study of the spirit and for the reality of the spirit in all of life. With her passing it was as though she was able to enfold each of the grandchildren from the other side in an embrace of radiating, spiritual warmth. She had loved her spiritual path, lived it and left a legacy of unwavering faith to family and friends. Though they would miss her greatly, for she had been a powerful presence in their lives, when she went into the next world it became a heralded event. She was home, and, thanks to anthroposophy, we had no doubt she knew where she was.

It came about like this. The life changing phone call came on a cold winter afternoon telling us she had died of an unexpected heart attack. Stunned, I gathered with the children in a group hug where we clung together with shock and grief. But within less than a moment our youngest, a six-year-old son danced out of the hug and emphatically proclaimed, "Grandma died but she's alive!" It was an announcement of absolute certainty, like a typical no-nonsense reminder from Lola herself declaring, "This is the truth of the matter, so don't forget it!"

Soon after my oldest daughter returned from work. When told about her grandmother, her face blanched in anguished disbelief and, sobbing, she rushed from the room. Though I longed to follow her, I felt I should respect her space to deal with it in her own way. I was astonished when she reappeared shortly and told us. "How can we be sad? Grandma is just saying 'Whoopie!'"

And so it went. Amidst our tears and grief these strong affirming statements continued to come from all her grandchildren and many friends. Our tall, lanky, teenaged son, Cameron, who would help the priest with her service, declared, "You know she is happy there and she gave happiness to everyone here. She was a wonderful woman so you just can't be sad about it."

Our oldest son, Gary, a fine wood craftsman, immediately began to make her casket and all his five siblings helped. The twins, Mary and Vivian, cleaned out their grandmother's closets, pausing to dress up and parade in a dozen get–ups that Lola would have loved. They cleaned house, made the guest book, hugged their bereft grandfather tenderly and often. Lola had taught them to love the elementals and all the treasures from the woods and now they made the house beautiful with lovely nature arrangements and placed stones and sprays of pine boughs and flowers in and around her casket for the ceremony to celebrate her life.

People are always concerned about the effect of death on children. Yet many small children can dreamily remember the spiritual world from which they came. Still star-spangled and angel-kissed, they inwardly know it is a reality, especially if those truths are echoed in the adults around them. Their fears of death or their acceptance of it are largely instilled over time by the adults around them. We can understand children can fear burial or abandonment, the death of the parents, or the fear that no one will be there to care for them and love them. All these concerns are alleviated when the adults can surround the children with courage and spiritual awareness, despite the grief, and hold onto the deeper faith in the situation.

My husband and I were determined that our six children be able to experience death as a natural part of life, and that the ending of life should have as much care and meaning as the welcoming of a new baby. With that resolve, we nursed two bedridden elders for over three years so they could die at home with us. We felt this part of family living was just as important as any life lesson. It bore fruit, for every one of our grown children has been able to be present for community deaths with the ability to give calm and competent help as needed. I might add that we limited our children's exposure to the countless gory, virtual reality deaths via media that are too often are children's education on the subject. Real life is not entertainment, but death comes as a major point of growth for our development, whatever our age, and warrants the awe and respect such suffering and transformation engenders.

As we supported other families to bring their loved ones home to die, our home death care work spread throughout our wider community. For me it grew to nationwide consulting and meetings with Elizabeth Kubler-Ross, the well-known authority on death and dying and to whom we owe so much in this field. She gave the blessing to carry on her work. I have since traveled across the country for over twenty-five years helping communities form threshold committees, giving conferences on the legal, practical, and spiritual aspects of home deaths, and eventually I was able to write a book to pass the knowledge on to others.

I was drawn to threshold work because I felt the final celebration of a human life should be beautiful, honoring the person's life as much as possible. It is the last great act of a person's life, when the eternal spirit triumphs over the mortal body. A person's death can be a gift to those left behind, for the dying individual opens the door to the spiritual world. Even amidst the sorrow and shock of a sudden death, spiritual grace and love can pour in for the families and for the community as it did for our family. The same grace is given when a baby is born into earthly life, opening the door for angels and lifting our lives and awareness to the mysteries between this world and the next.

To be sure, community work at the threshold needs to be carried with a lot of common sense and awareness of the multiple levels of support needed by the survivors. The ensuing farewells are not only for the one who has died, but are major life transitions for the whole family. As supporters we need to be sensitive to what is best for each one involved. But in general, the more the surviving loved ones are able to participate, (prayer, helping bathe and dress the body, making a guest book, helping with biography for the eulogy, arranging pictures, placing flowers in the casket, etc.) the sooner the healing process can begin. At a home death, the conscious attentive help of friends is invaluable for the family adjusting to the new situation.

The deep spiritual truths of life and death can come to us as precious gifts from the children. I feel that children often led us back to the universal wholeness of the cycles of life. During my years as a kindergarten teacher, I taught a sweet, breezy, four-year-old girl who was devastated when her beloved grandmother died. But the next day she was her cheerful self. Her grandmother had appeared to her in a dream and the girl then confidently proclaimed her grandmother would be back. Most counselors see this as childhood denial and wishful thinking, which it can be. But it can also be a child's direct experience of spiritual worlds and the great concepts of reincarnation. I urged her family to support her confident view but, if asked, be indefinite about the time of coming back.

Rudolf Steiner tells us, ". . . we have in us as a reality that part of us which bears the individual entity of the human being and which will carry it through the gate of death, through the spiritual world, and once again into a new earthly life."

The children consistently echo his initiate knowledge in their own direct and charming language.

My young grandson tells me, "When you die, you go back to heaven and then God gives you a new body." Another first grader announced, "We only own our spirits, our bodies come from God."

A six-year-old consoles her mother, "I know you're worried, Mama, because you are wearing out. But it's all right. When you die you'll go and hold hands with the angels and God will give you a brand new body so you can come back again."

A four-year-old boy told his mother, "First I chose you and then I had to find Dad in a hurry and a long way away and bring him to you so I could be borned."

When our youngest son was six he climbed in bed one morning, fresh from sleep, and had this conversation with his father:

"This is my eighth family!"
"How do you know?" his father asked.
"I counted' em. My first was Egypt, I think."
"How can your remember?"
"The fairies saved my heart so I can remember," he replied with shining eyes.

A little girl whose father died comforted her mother with this timeless wisdom saying, "Daddy has finished his tasks on earth and has taken them to heaven as gifts."

This knowledge in children comes from deep wells of remembrance of the time when we were one with the spiritual world before setting off on our journey's to earthly individuality, isolation, freedom, and choice. They know with eternal wisdom that life follows death as surely as God is love and summer follows winter. They long for the confidence and security of knowing we know that too.

When my husband's beloved grandmother died in our home, we had a home vigil and her body lay in the same room where I taught kindergarten for many years. Grandma had always loved the children and with her passing more than a hundred and twenty adults and children came for their first experience of death—Grandma's final gift to the community. While still a confronting experience for many, the setting was warm and inviting, filled with family vitality and naturalness, children playing outside, adults visiting in the kitchen, others reading for Grandma in her new life.

One young mother who had never seen death, came to honor Grandma. But she left her two-year-old son in the car just by the door as she came in to briefly pay her respects. She wanted to shield the boy from a fearful experience. She came into the sunny room, filled with a warm pink glow from the magenta curtains, with hesitant and reverent steps. With a deep breath she was just taking it in when her son escaped from the car and burst into the room. His mother was startled and embarrassed. But the two-year-old would have none of it. He ran to the casket and grasped one of the handles and tried to rock it. His mother was mortified, but I just laughed. "It's just fine, that is Grandma's cradle and you can rock it for her," I told him. The mother relaxed and the lively boy eagerly investigated each flower, rock and picture in the room. Then it was time to
go and the mother lifted the child up into her arms. Now for the first time he could see the body in the casket. But he gave it only a cursory glance. Then looking heavenward he addressed the palpable spiritual presence of Grandma that filled the room. With great smiles and shining eyes, he joyfully waved his chubby fingers and repeatedly said, "Bye-bye, bye-bye!" The mother was astounded and I laughed with the sheer wonder of watching his direct connection with the spirit, not the body. Yes, a little child shall lead us!

Another demonstration of the children's beautiful connection with the spirit, occurred when my father, called Pappy by his grandchildren, died with us at home. Again, many came for his vigil, including a family with a six-year-old son. The boy sat on his father's lap beside the casket where my father's body lay, while his father read him a lively children's story that the boy was obviously enjoying. They came back the next day as well, and again I remarked the child's unusual joy and enthusiasm. The family moved to another state and I lost track of them. But over twenty years later I was in a conference in their town and stayed with the family. While I was there, their son called home and the mother identified me as the visitor who was "Pappy's daughter." "Pappy!" the now young man exclaimed with all the joy of one remembering a treasured old friend from his childhood. But here is the amazing thing. He had never met my father while Pappy was still in physical life. They truly "met" while Pappy was vibrantly alive in the surrounding spirit. That powerful and amazing meeting, spirit to spirit, had warmed the boy's life and memory from that time on.

Our children can remind us of the gifts and the mystery of the threshold and the amazing dance of souls between the seen and unseen world—souls being released from their physical bodies into the cosmic freedom of the spiritual world, and those gathering their life intentions to descend into earthly birth and the narrow confines of the physical body. Our innocent and open children, fresh from the universe, can quicken our hearts with such knowing too.

Nancy Jewel Poer is a co-founder of Rudolf Steiner College and has been a faculty member there for nearly thirty years, teaching American Studies and Child Development. She founded three Waldorf kindergartens, the last becoming the Cedar Springs Waldorf School in Placerville, California. She lectures nationwide and is known for her Waldorf parenting work as well as her pioneering book, Living Into Dying, A Journal of Spiritual and Practical Deathcare for Family and Community. *She is a mother of six and a grandmother of twelve.*

A Festival for a Threshold Crossing

Patricia Owens

The birthday celebration in the kindergarten is a rare and almost sacred event in the life of the child and his or her parents. Tears of joy well in many parents' eyes during the story as they are reminded of the spiritual journey that has brought their child to earth and into their arms. Each child, still so fresh from the spiritual world, savors the story of the *Rainbow Bridge* and beams with wisdom and delight. Reviewing the deeds of each year is a recognition of their intentions for this lifetime. Every birthday is a joyous and solemn occasion, which in its simplicity also has profound depth. I always sense their fascination and joy in one another's birthdays. It is as if they are remembering that their classmates have chosen to again be with them on the earth. Truly, the children are filled with the inner knowing of their connection to their spiritual home. This is one festival that adults can no longer experience in the same way as the children who may retain those "intimations of immortality." It is with this understanding and insight, I wish to share the following "festival" that was conceived and born during the Holy Nights.

On the morning of December 26 a beautiful blanket of snow graced the earth. With this Christmas gift from the heavens also came the shocking news that my colleague Peggy Burns had suddenly crossed the threshold. With stunned disbelief, calls to kindergarten parents were made and a substitute was chosen within hours. Later that evening, I carried a perfectly bloomed amaryllis (that had gloriously opened that morning) to Peggy's classroom to meet my colleagues. To our amazement, we found her room perfectly cleaned, arranged, and cleared of all Advent decorations. Peggy had hosted a potluck gathering for the parents and children of her class on the last day prior to vacation. As she was a new teacher at the school, and most of the families were new to the school, she encouraged a wonderful social bonding. She was the only teacher at Green Meadow who celebrated with families on this day. This joyous holiday party was a labor of love attended by all of her children and parents. It was her final goodbye.

When I entered her room that day I felt eerily empty. I lit a candle and began with a Hallelujah in eurythmy as an offering to her soul. As the teachers performed the repetitive gestures together, we could sense her presence and our connection. We enlisted her help from the spiritual world and shared our thoughts. We read aloud from the St. Luke Gospel. Nothing more could be said. We carried Peggy, the children, and their parents into our sleep on this Holy Night.

The questions and concerns for the children were obvious. How could we make their transition as natural as possible? How could we help transform the grief of the devoted parents so visibly shaken by this shock? How could we ourselves face the daunting tasks that lay ahead? The comfort was in knowing that the spiritual world would guide us.

Inwardly, I carried the children and continued my nightly readings throughout the Holy Nights. I was in contact with another colleague as to our plans for Peggy's class. The kindergarten teachers and the parents agreed that a visit to the classroom, prior to the scheduled school day, would serve to ease the transition for the children. It would be short and simple, and most importantly, it was to be a celebration!

For one week prior to the festival the new teacher, Christiane Landowne, worked to ensoul the room with her own touches. Then, on Sunday, January 5, we held a very unique and memorable "festival" in the kindergarten classroom. All the kindergarten teachers arrived to ready the space and prepare refreshments, expectant yet tentative, putting emotions aside. An important task was at hand. How would it be for the children to enter their classroom and not be greeted by their beloved Mrs. Burns?

The teachers greeted the children and their parents with soft voices and welcoming smiles. As usual, they hung up their coats on their own hooks. Familiar faces surrounded them—faces that the children recognized from the playground and puppet shows. Silently they drifted about the room and slowly found seats on chairs, tables, and laps. Wide-eyed four- and five-year-olds appeared calmly reserved and thoughtful. Their parents were teary-eyed and uneasy, filled with anticipation of what was to come. A candle was lit and a story begun.

The story, *Birth into the Spiritual World* by Nancy Blanning, gave a beautiful picture of metamorphosis and homecoming. The story brought the image of a mother and child reunion, the most comforting of all archetypes. It was healing for us all. The shift of energy in the room was palpable. The tension seemed to melt away while the breathing of the children deepened as they entered the pictorial world. The story gave a glimpse into the invisible world of spirit. Through those words and images, the children could connect their experience, not in an abstract way, but as a living reality.

These same children, who together walked the Advent Spiral a month before, had experienced the light that can penetrate all darkness. The familiar birthday story now had another chapter that celebrated a joyous reunion. Two strengthening images were brought through the story. Two recent festivals had laid a foundation for this new Spiritual Birthday Festival!

After the candle was snuffed, the children sat down at the tables where sheets of beeswax had been laid. One teacher demonstrated the transformation of the flat sheet into a candle. They were quietly shown how to place the string (wick) at one end and begin rolling their very own candle to be taken home and light the way for their dear teacher. An array of rainbow colors accompanied sparkling eyes and bright smiles. They were then given more beeswax to decorate a large white candle for a centerpiece for the table. The children and their parents were
eager to oblige and the room began to hum with chatter and giggles as they sculpted their offerings. Soon the large candle was proudly decorated with stars, butterflies, symbols, and rainbows. Here they were again, happily busy at their kindergarten table in lively company. And now, did it truly feel like a celebration!

At this time Christiane Landowne entered into the room as had been planned. When one child noticed her familiar presence, he ran with a hug, "And here's our new teacher!" The timing could not have been more perfect and she was greeted with enthusiasm. Refreshments were served, parents mingled, and the teachers all breathed a deep sigh of relief, as the room filled with warmth, love, and peace, just as it had been on that last December celebration. Our hearts were lightened!

Through this experience, I was able to witness how the young child was able to come to an understanding through a living experience. Having been given an age-appropriate pictorial story to which they could relate, they were able to come to peace with a harsh reality. Working out of their will, they were able to participate in an artistic activity that was meaningful.

In reflecting on this unique, relatively unformed festival, I can say that its success was rooted in the groundwork of spiritual study and trust in the ever-present help of the spiritual World. What had transpired lives in the hearts of those children.

A few days later we overheard, "We have two teachers now, because Mrs. Burns looks down on us from heaven". How I had experienced knowing Peggy in her relationship with the children was a precious gift. Her gifts continue.

Patricia Owens, a trained eurythmist and Waldorf early childhood educator, currently works with the nursery children at Green Meadow Waldorf School in New York. She wrote this essay for an assignment on festivals during her Waldorf Early Childhood training at Sunbridge College.

Birth Into The Spiritual World

Nancy Blanning

A woman who had planted a beautiful garden found a caterpillar in her garden one day. She took it home and placed it gently in a dish by her bedside. At night the caterpillar would sing to her and the singing caused her to dream. She dreamed of the meadow from which all children come. There, in her dream, she saw a woman she dimly remembered and finally recognized as the Mother of the Meadow, in whose lap she had rocked long ago. Each night she dreamed of the meadow and the Mother and dreamed that the woman was calling to her, asking her to return to her lap, as she had been away so long. When she awoke each morning the memory of her dream became stronger and stronger and she also felt herself grow more and more tired and less able to tend the garden she had so carefully planted and cared for. At last one night in her dream she said to the Mother that she would like to come to the meadow, but she could not leave her garden for who would care for it? The Mother answered that she had been the only one who could have planted the garden, but there were other loving gardeners who would nurture her flowers and help them grow into beautiful strong plants. At last the woman said, "Yes, I will come, but how can I travel such a great distance when I am so tired and am no longer strong?" The Mother told her that the secret lay at her side, and she saw that the caterpillar had transformed itself into a beautiful butterfly with wings so vast they could carry her anywhere. She had one more question before she climbed onto the butterfly's back. "Can I never come back and visit my garden and beautiful flowers? How can I find my way back?" The Mother answered, "Yes, you may come back. Whenever those who have known you and loved you light a candle and remember you, that light will shine across the vast distance and show you the way back. You can speak to them in your dreams and they will know that you have been nearby." So she mounted the back of the butterfly and flew up into the great, starry sky. When she reached the meadow the Mother wrapped her arms about the woman, who had again become small like a tiny baby. "Today is your birthday in the meadow and for that we celebrate."

Nancy Blanning is the remedial and therapeutic teacher at the Denver Waldorf School and prior to that taught seventeen years in the preschool/kindergarten.

Story for Mia

Louise De Forest

The image of the golden horse inspired a tale told by Green Meadow kindergarten teachers, when a former student, who had moved to New Zealand, fell from a horse and was killed. She was known by many of the kindergarten children and the teachers describe their story and the children's response in their newsletter. Mia, five years old, died in New Zealand in a riding accident. When I told the story to my kindergartners, many of whom are friends of Mia's, there was great rejoicing among the children. How their faces beamed thinking of Mia living with the angels and they actually laughed and clapped their hands. How cruel the death of a child seems to us adults; our faith is sorely tested at moments like these and we grieve for the parents and family and wonder why these things have to happen. And yet for these four and five year olds, so much closer to other realities than we are, there was an understanding that Mia had gone back home.

One morning Mia awoke and said to herself, "Today I will ride a golden horse." And when it came time for her riding lesson, there was the golden horse waiting for her. The golden horse stumbled and fell and so did Mia and the angels came and helped her get up and they took Mia to live with them. Now Mia can be with all her friends whenever she wants to and she will come and play with you in your dreams.

Louis DeForest is a Waldorf early childhood educator at Green Meadow Waldorf School in Spring Valley, NY. She has also been involved in adult education, parent counseling, and is helping to develop Waldorf early childhood teacher education in Mexico.

Grandma's Dream

Sheila Rubin

Grandma's faith was a personal one, built not on doctrine, but on her own experience. Her dreams held the deepest significance for her, and conveyed to her a certainty both of life beyond this physical one and of the bonds of love which transcend death. But these fruits came to her gradually in her life and not without great anguish.

My grandmother was a happily married young woman when she delivered her much-awaited first child. The baby was breech, and she was in labor for many long hours. When, after great difficulty, he was finally born, his umbilical cord was wrapped around his neck so tightly that it had strangled him. It was a terrible tragedy—the army doctor, who had done his best to assist her, sat down on the bed and wept. A year later, she and her husband found the courage to try again, and my uncle Sandy was born, assuaging the sharpest of her grief. Still, the memory of that first little boy never left her.

Years after she had borne and lost her baby, she had a dream. She was in the midst of a wonderful procession, at the side of her sister Blanche (who had died years before, as a young woman). It was glorious, everyone was singing joyfully together as they walked, but Grandma was a bit puzzled. "Blanche," she whispered, "Where are we going?" "Don't you know?" Blanche answered. "We're going to see God." Just then a radiant little boy ran up to Grandma and threw his arms around her knees. He seemed familiar, but she couldn't quite remember from where. "Blanche, he's so beautiful, but who is he?" "Oh Maudie, don't you know? He's your little boy that died!"

As Grandma told me this dream her eyes overflowed with tears. "I don't know why it always makes me cry," she said. "It was the happiest dream I ever had."

Sheila Rubin teaches at the Redmont School in Birmingham, Alabama. This true story has given the author help and strength through her own loss, and has been a great help to those parents facing a loss with whom she has shared the story. It would not necessarily be shared with young children.

For Anastasia and Her Dear Grandmother Who Crossed the Threshold at Advent

Cynthia Aldinger

Once upon a time not very long ago,
A dear little family loved each other so,
That they created a wish that went traveling far,
Until at last it went up to the stars.

In the heavens the star children worked all day on matters of great importance. When they had worked very hard, they were given the gift of beautiful music—so beautiful that it brought great joy to their hearts. Sometimes, when they were not working or listening to the music, they were able to play heavenly games like Catch a Falling Star or Chase a Comet's Tail.

One day a star child went running so fast
That she came to the edge of the heavens at last.
And when she gazed down to the Earth below
The wish wrapped around her and started to grow.
She went straight to her angel and said, with a vow,
"I must go to the Earth to begin my work now."
For when she'd looked down, she'd seen the same
Dear little family from whom the wish came.

The star child was delighted by the amazing sight she saw, for there waiting for her were a mother, a father, a brother, and a sister and other loving family and friends. When she went to her angel, her angel looked at her and looked at her and finally said, "But dear one, you still have much work to do here in the heavens."

The little star child said, "Oh, please, may I go, if only for a little while. I won't stay long, and perhaps I will bring someone special back with me."

The angels gathered together to consider the special request of the little star child and, at last, decided to grant her her wish.

Then all of the heavenly angels did sing.
And the guardian angel said, "Here, I'll take your wings.
I'll keep them here safely until you return.
Now, go to the Earth and learn all you can learn."

Then all the star children gathered quite near
To say "good-bye" to their friend so dear
And as she climbed down from Heaven's high ridge,
She started across the rainbow bridge.

Now, on her journey, the star child saw the most wondrous sight, for there before her she could see a radiant being who was gathering light from the sun, moon and stars and tucking the light into her beautiful blue cloak as she went along. It was the mother of the Child of Light, the Christ Child, who every year made her journey through the heavens down to the earth to weave a garment of light for her Son. Also tucked into her cloak and all about her were many star children who were coming to the Earth as well so that they could come to know this special Son.

"Oh," thought the littlest star child, "How

I would love to be wrapped in that mantle of blue some day when I journey back to the heavens," for such was the case that every year the Lady also allowed some children to journey back with her upon her return. Then the littlest star child closed her eyes and fell into a dream of such a time when that could happen.

And when she awoke, another amazing sight was there before her. She had come all the way across the rainbow bridge and was now in the home of the dear little family she had seen from the heavens. How happy they all were that she had come.

In time, the little child grew from a baby to a toddler to a lovely little girl who loved to laugh and play. Her family loved her dearly, and her grandmother sometimes cared for her when the others had to be away. Soon it was that special time of year again when many star children come near the Earth waiting for their time to be born while others prepare for their return wrapped in the mantel of blue. The little girl could dimly remember the splendor of the heavens and, without even knowing it, yearned for the sounds of the joyful music.

The angels called to the little girl that the time had come for her return. Her grandmother, who loved her dearly, carried her up to the heavens where the radiant Mother wrapped them both in her mantle of blue, and they were clothed in the light of the sun, moon and stars. Though they were sad to leave behind their family and friends, they knew that they would all be together again one day.

And in the heavens, there was great rejoicing.

Cynthia Aldinger of Lifeways North America wrote this story for a young family whose two children were in the kindergarten class of one of her students. Ms. Aldinger had been visiting the class the day the three-year-old child and her grandmother were killed in an automobile accident.

The Inner Path

Self–Development as a Basis for the Relationship between the Child and the Adult

Michaela Glöckler, M.D.

The closer a child is to birth, the less individualized he is. Babies are similar to each other and easy to mix up. A care–giver, relating to a group of infants, will have more difficulty in recognizing them from one another, than for instance if he or she had been relating to a group of elderly people, where the individual personality is very pronounced. The little child lacks self-consciousness; the individuality is not yet born. We meet the child in this delicate phase of life, where he possesses qualities that can be called *generally human.*

Because of this, it is essential that we as care–givers generate our most powerful general human qualities. And if we ask ourselves what is meant by generally human, the answer is to be found in that realm which is accessible to everyone, regardless of age, language, or background. We meet in the realm of sense perception, where a gesture or a smile of joy is recognized by anyone. In our daily life, and in caring for the daily rhythms, we move in the realm of what is generally human. This also belongs to our life of thought, our gestures, and our speech. The little child is open towards everything that surrounds it, and therefore it is essential that our consciousness penetrate this realm of generally human qualities, in which the child lives. We must learn to generalize ourselves and to meet the child without expectations or prejudices. As caregivers we can sometimes do this better than parents. It is also essential that one has love for those whom one cares for, and here we have a big advantage, for it is easier at first to love a baby than, for instance, a teenager.

Practicing self–discipline in the realm of thinking, speaking and doing is essential, as these penetrate and color the daily life of the child. In the realm of thinking, this is the search for truth. It is important to observe thinking, and to see how every thought has its own truth, its own reality. Thoughts serve each other, penetrate and carry each other. We must learn to purify our thinking, to discern what is really true, irrespective of our own opinion.

Our thoughts live in our speech, colored by our life of feeling, and they also influence our deeds. We must consider if our intentions are relevant, so that our deeds fit the need. Is my deed healing or destructive? We must learn to look at our "good" deeds also from their shadow sides. For instance, you all think it is very good that you are attending this conference, but for those at home it may be a very bad thing, because there we have left things undone. Can I carry the consequences of my deeds? And does my speech reflect not only what is true and what I intend to do, but also carry warmth and love for the children?

We can discern three aspects of our speech:

Thinking: "Is what I say true?"—Truth

Feeling: "Does it express what lives in my heart?"—Love

Willing: "Can I be trusted to stand for what I say?"—Freedom

We are speaking here of the most delicate and precious human substance, which is an expression of how the Christ lives with us. It is like a handshake with Christ each day, when we say "yes" to living out of these three qualities of truth, love and freedom.

Rudolf Steiner described three paths of self-development: the personal, the professional and the generally human one. The personal path is described in *How to Know Higher Worlds,* and is the individual way. In following this path, one can have a "taste" of egoism. Regarding the professional path of schooling, Steiner has given different indications for those who take up the tasks of a healer, an artist, an educator, and so on. These paths are followed to develop faculties to help others, and are selfless paths.

The third path is the generally human path, where we must develop ourselves, so that we feel more and more a part of humanity in general. What is the purpose and meaning of what is happening in the world today, at the end of the century? How do I deal with the evil that is *growing* in the world around us, not only in wars, destruction and killing, but also in the social life and in meetings between people. We must work to recognize and combat misunderstanding. The forces of evil are so strong at present, and we must learn what their message to our self-development is.

As a counter-picture to all this evil and destruction, Steiner tells us that mankind is crossing the threshold to the spiritual world. Killing takes place in the world around us, where the battle is not taken up inwardly. Killing is in its place when we overcome something the shadows hide of ourselves. When we use the power to overcome, to conquer something within ourselves, we are then able to project peace outside ourselves. Meeting the questions of our time in this way, becomes a real path of schooling. Steiner himself has called his book, *How to Know Higher Worlds,* an "anti-war book."

When we look at the little child, who is incarnating into the realm of what is generally human, we must look at its development of the senses. This touches an important aspect of the professional path in the light of developing generally human qualities. In the first seven years the child lives more strongly in the four lower senses. From seven to fourteen he lives strongly in the middle senses, and incarnates between ages fourteen to twenty-one in the higher senses.

The way in which we give support to the development of the lower senses in the early years, is essential to the development of the higher senses in adolescence. We have in our hands the capacity to help or to hinder individual development through what is generally human. The way in which the child incarnates in the four lower senses of touch, life, movement and balance, creates the organs whereby he later can develop the senses of ego, thought, word and hearing. The way in which the care–giver lives through her higher senses, influences and forms the child as he incarnates in the lower senses.

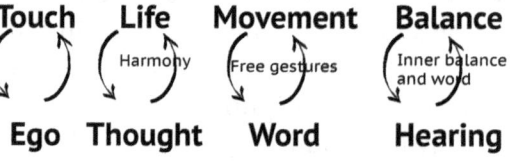

(The downward arrow indicates the relationship between the child's lower senses and the later development of the higher senses. The upward arrow indicates how the adult's being works upon the child.)

- The sense of *touch* is the precondition for

the development of the sense of *I* or *Ego* of the other person.

- Sense of *life* develops the sense organs in the child, whereby he can later perceive the *thoughts* of *others*.

- Development of the sense of *movement* is essential for the development of *speech* and the sense of *word*.

- Balance and inner calm are the preconditions for development of the sense of *hearing*.

What must the educator develop to support the development of the four lower senses of the child? He must cultivate self-experience through the twelve senses, regarding the gifts he wins through sense–experience.

The following description addresses the way in which the child incarnates in the lower senses, and how the adult can aid this process, realizing the gifts, which are the results of sense–experience in his own being.

Touch

Touch gives self-awareness, an experience of our bodily form and self-existence. Other people carrying and caring for us nurture this experience. Babies need cuddling, the care–giver must be sensitive to the individual child's need and respond to that. Some children want less contact than others. A baby who cries a lot may have difficulty incarnating in the lower body, and may be helped by leg and foot massage. In the little child the sense of touch and the sense of I are still one, and only develop separately after the age of three. The ego sense of the adult is essential in establishing good social surroundings and the care of the child. Any form of abuse—lack of ego presence where the animal drives come to the fore—is more damaging at this age than at any other age.

Life

To stimulate the child's sense of life, the social sense, one must care for the daily rhythms, the preparing and giving of meals, sleeping and so on, in a harmonious way. For children who come from a home where there may be a lot of noise or disharmony, it is of great importance to experience harmony and peace in the adults' manner of relating to one another.

Movement

The children must have the possibility to move freely—in this lies the development of freedom. The bodily experience of freedom is the basis for the later experience of being a free human being. The adult's gestures and words influence the child's movement development, our spontaneity and joy have a positive influence on the child, whereas untrue words make the child un–free in its movements.

Balance

The little child should be allowed to roll and climb about in all possible positions, so that the sense of balance can develop. (It would be a good thing from time to time to invite a Bothmer gymnast to observe the children in their play. She would have the possibility to recognize any movement disturbances very early, and possibly recommend treatment to the parents if this is necessary.) The adult's inner peace and balance, knowing when to interfere and when not, is essential.

Where trust (sense of touch), harmony, freedom and the inner balance are established in the growing young person, drug abuse becomes impossible. This can only come about where these qualities are lacking.

The guiding motive of the first seven years of the child is that of the Father God. The child lives in the realm of the Creator

Being, the giver of the senses and sense perception. The child must experience that the world is good. If we can, establish child–care centers where this is possible, then we can together with the parent's care at home, provide the best possible basis for the child's healthy development.

Questions and Answers:

Q: What do you mean "war inside/war outside?"

A: We are at the end of the first third of the three periods of development of the consciousness soul. Through the deed of Golgotha, the death and resurrection of the Christ, man was for the first time able to carry his I consciousness through the death experience, and this I development continues. Christ did not only bring peace, but also the strengthening of the *I* experience, and along with this comes egoism. (Rudolf Steiner, *Gospel of St. Luke,* Chapter 12)

In our epoch the struggle is with evil. The old traditions carry us no longer, and we must therefore develop our higher ego qualities. This situation will last into the seventh Post Atlantean epoch (about 7,700 AD), where it will be a war of all against all. Waldorf education is based on altruism and the developing of general human qualities. These are necessary as a counter balance to the development of individualism.

Q: Who comes first—the mother or the child?

A: As caregivers, of course, our first concern is the child. We must "take on" the mother as well and not try to educate her. If we do, we only increase her guilty conscience. We must give her joy in her child, tell her about small, wonderful experiences with her child and make her happy about him. If we succeed in making her so happy about him that she gives up her job, so as not to miss being with him, then we have been really successful! If she herself feels confident enough to ask questions, we can then answer these. The most important thing is to support her in feeling she is a good mother. We must make the mother happy, as the child thrives on joy!

Try to establish routines for the children as much as possible without change. If changes are necessary, make them after a half or a whole year. The following holds true regarding human rhythm:

Ego—24–hour rhythm,
Astral—7–day rhythm,
Etheric—1–month rhythm,
Physical—1–year rhythm.

We should also make a list of problems as well as suggestions for solutions. It would be good to find people prepared to specialize in studying each year itself. During the first third of each period the child is most vulnerable, for example:

First year (of a three–year period),
First four months (of the first year),
First three months (of a pregnancy).

Q: What about vaccination?

A: Steiner spoke about vaccination, which at the time was only against smallpox. He said that spiritual development in the adult is the only way to combat the negative effects. Vaccinations weaken the immune system and the ego development. To combat this, we must fill ourselves with love, idealism, joy, enthusiasm, religion and culture.

Q: Can you say more about how the astral body of the educator works in the etheric body of the child?

A: We speak about the Pedagogical Law, which Steiner gives in Lecture 2 of his *Curative Course.* The Pedagogical Law is that the higher body of the teacher influences the next lower body of the child:

What lives in the ego of the teacher works upon the astral body of the child.

What lives in the astral of the teacher works upon the etheric body of the child.

What lives in the etheric of the teacher works upon the physical body of the child.

What the teacher creates in the physical is part of the child's destiny.

When the teacher works with his ego, he stimulates the astral body of the child with light and warmth. The adult's work with the Subsidiary Exercises influences his astral body, and has a positive effect on the children. It is then easy to establish good habits. Rhythm, repeating things, strengthens the etheric body and also the physical body. Flaws, or basic moods from one life which have not been overcome, influence the next lower body in our next life. The karma we carry in our astral, etheric, and physical bodies is formed through our past lives. However, in our ego we don't carry impressions from past lives, there we are free and can work to overcome, to transform and to heal our past. In developing our ego capacity we can gain power to bring the Pedagogical Law into effect.

Dr. Michaela Glöckler is currently the head of the Medical Section of the School of Spiritual Science in Dornach, Switzerland. She has been active as a pediatrician and school doctor in Germany and is the author of A Guide to Child Health, *Floris Books. This article from a lecture given February 1998 during first international anthroposophical conference on "The Care of the Little Child" held in Odense, Denmark, was taken from notes by Barbara Paulsen, and was revised by the lecturer. For further understanding, Michaela Glockler recommends her booklet* Begabung and Behinderung *in which aspects of the pedagogical law and self-experience in the twelve senses are described*

Through the Eye of the Needle
Felicitas Vogt

How do we go through the eye of the needle to find new forms when the old ways no longer hold us and something new must be born?

When we look around at our time—at the pressures, the attacks on our lives—we can speak of a number of wounds that are increasingly prominent in our everyday life. The first wound results from the decrease in the power of old social forms. We long for encounter with others; we yearn for communication. Yet instead, we increase our social isolation and aggression against one another. We live in war against each other. It is strenuous to break through this isolation, to really meet the other human being. It is a consolation to read Rudolf Steiner, for he suggests that this phenomenon, the fact that it is more and more difficult to meet the other soul in one's own inner being, belongs to the development of the consciousness soul. This process is a general irritation today. We feel the old forces decreasing as the power of past social settings and securities is lost, and the new inner forces are not yet there in full strength.

Every day we experience the struggle to become an independent ego, a human being standing on our own feet. And it seems to become even harder to fight against all that would hinder us from standing upright.

Adults as well as children even fight against help, because help can make us dependent upon the helper. We somehow know that we must stand alone. This has the effect of producing the well-known quality of social and societal autism. The second wound that we live with today is the combination of lack of self-esteem and workaholicism. In Europe, in 1999, there was a very large conference of psychotherapists and psychologists, which began with this statement: Over eighty percent of people living in Europe suffer from a lack of self-confidence and self-esteem. This is an important statement. Social conflicts arise when I don't have self-esteem. I need to be seen as a good person, so I criticize others to feel good about myself. Look at modern advertising: "Treat yourself to something good." "Indulge yourself." The message is, "I am worth it; I should use this perfume." Coming out of this lack of self-esteem, we have more and more workaholics. When I work and work and work, I feel I have the right to live, that I am worthy of living.

What do these characteristics do inside of us individually? Due to lack of self-esteem we start to wear masks, images of ourselves, which must always be positive—or always negative, as in "I can't do anything right." Of course, these masks are not true images, but as we identify with them—suffering, weak, joyful, grateful individuals—cease to know who we really are. This produces vast distances between us and other individuals.

The third wound is that of fixed ideas and perceptions. In our living from morning to night we have a fixed perception of how reality has to be, how a Waldorf kindergarten program, for instance, has to be. These rigid ideas hold us, for when I am fixed I don't have to be as flexible as the situation demands of me. These hardened perceptions are a kind of poison.

Our fourth wound is instant judgment. By practicing instant judgments without having taken in what is being talked about, we are led in a vicious circle back to fixed perception.

We create our fifth wound by blaming others and blaming circumstances. In our time we all suffer on a social level and it is a great temptation to blame others for the situation. We blame the circumstances. We develop this blaming as a coping mechanism, but it is an illusion.

The sixth wound in our modern life is reliance on group opinions. Standing on our own feet is a strenuous exercise that must be practiced every day. It is easy to relax this effort, and we sometimes like to fall back into group opinions. We must find our own opinions. Individualized anthroposophy is the only thing that will carry us into the next millennium. It is not enough to rely on the anthroposophy we read in lectures. We have to work through it individually.

Our seventh wound is that of materialism. In the insecurity of our times, we are tempted to bolster our dignity by surrounding ourselves with material things. Many people build themselves up with products. The thinking, feeling, and willing of our human soul becomes bound to the past through being bound to material things.

This brings us to an important fact of our lives: we are exhausted. These behaviors, these wounds, use up our life forces. When we live in society today, our energy diminishes. This dwindling is one problem in our practical work as teachers. We don't have the forces, the enthusiastic joy for our children anymore, and we call the children "more difficult."

Before birth, human souls see what is happening now on the earth—the materialism, the cold technological environment around human beings. These souls say "yes" to this and enter this world in order to help the world change. When they meet us, seeing exhausted and burned-out kindergarten teachers and parents, they have great difficulty, but they can't express it. For the children who are coming onto the earth know how to save and rescue the world. They have this teaching, coming from the spiritual world. But when we try to make them fit into our system, our life and society, we kill their spiritual path.

The question is: Are we flexible enough to change kindergartens and homes in order to meet the needs of children today? The way children are nourished has changed completely. The children are hungry. They are physically, emotionally, and spiritually malnourished. The children need a different, specific and individual approach from us. They need life forces from us.

We are faced with individualities who have difficulty penetrating subjects. In Germany, the Ritalin program for ADHD is increasingly popular. Certain children with organic problems do need Ritalin; it is a good transitional coping mechanism. But it is a crime against the soul of a child to administer Ritalin to him to make him fit better into his classroom and into our school system. Children can't develop other than they do in our medicated, media-filled culture.

They are very often hyperactive because of the culture; then we give them a biochemical bomb (Ritalin) to concentrate in front of the computer.

The real remedy for many of these children would be the warm attention of adults and stimuli for the lower senses. But we can only create this in our kindergartens when we have life forces, and instead we are suffering from a sort of everlasting soul influenza. When we have the flu physically, we separate ourselves, put ourselves to bed, and pull the blankets up. We don't want to see anybody. We need quiet, silence, and rest, for our life forces are needed to overcome this illness. We might say, "Not one more problem." "I can't cope with these parents." These are signs of this perpetual soul flu. When I am out of life forces I cannot encounter the spiritual being of the individual child. To encounter the other human being I have to go out of myself, toward the other. This is a kind of sacrifice.

Nature of the I

Rudolf Steiner, in *The Apocalypse of St. John,* says that the human I has two aspects. One is bound to the past, to the remembrance of security and fixed perceptions. This was good in former times. The other aspect, the social aspect of the I, is able to live with others and can connect with the spiritual qualities of a community. In *Against the Pollution of the I,* Jacques Lusseyran suggests that the malady of non-communication is a progressive poison. By giving the lower ego free rein, the I is put to death. The I is fragile.

It won't be easy to come to the I. It will be a fight, a battle inside us. But if we don't fight this battle, other forces will enter us. Those who do fight will come to powerlessness, will feel: "I don't know anymore. I don't know anything. I don't want to know anything."

This desperation is itself the eye of the needle. This is a moment when we have to say "yes." To say "yes" to this zero-point is a step on the path of initiation. It is a step I cannot take on my own, but a spiritual being must help me, for I can no longer do anything; there is nothing coming from the world anymore. Development always means going through this point of suffering and powerlessness.

It seems that human beings can manage anything these days—we can manipulate genes and affect the stock exchange. The power of intelligence is incredible today. But the meeting of materialistic and spiritual power always involves passage through the eye of the needle. The more I am connected to the material world, the more there is a need to connect with the spiritual world in order to stay with the course of human development.

When I am angry with a person, when tears come, there is a dissolution of things. Tears are a beautiful picture of the softening of the material world. The best sign of a new solution is tears! So let us cry for something starts to move when I cry. The moment I begin to cry is already one part of the solution. The moment I go through the eye of the needle, I will perceive the world differently, as processes. I will be wiser and milder. These are the qualities of old people. This soft way of looking at the way things are going on in the world is one of the beautiful results of going through the eye of the needle. You have no need to judge a situation anymore. You can relax. Ongoing judging is a sign of stress. You fix the world and use your life forces.

There are three qualities we have to develop inside us to go through the eye of the needle, to go through and not die or give up. To go through with confidence, without desperation, we need the qualities of wonder, compassion, and conscience.

Strengthening the Life Forces: How can we not only preserve the life forces in our four sheaths, but care for and develop them?

First of all, love and well–intended interest strengthen the life forces. Just loving the human beings around us, building up interest in everything and everybody just as they are, this brings life forces to the ego. It is important for our children to meet with and be stimulated by many things and diverse situations. This makes the I strong. The quality of loving the world as it is can then arise in puberty.

Love for the world is enhanced by well-intended interest in the spiritual being of the other. This is interest not in his mistakes but in those qualities that are perhaps not fully developed. Have you been in situations in which you are around certain people and you were better than you usually are? These people believed in you; they wanted to empower you. Usually we fix others in their mistakes, and this decreases life forces. But well-intended interest in the other makes everything better.

Secondly, we must seek to understand life processes, to know more clearly the relationship between human beings and world phenomena. For example, if we do not look deeply into the relationship between the development of the computer and the unfolding of the Michaelic stream, and we just say the computer is bad, we miss the connection, and our life forces decrease.

When we see how life processes work in the world, we may be better able to understand the different beings of boys and girls. Why is aggression increasing among boys while this is less the case in girls? We know that men and boys suffer most today. Why? Masculine power is used to manage and control. But you can't manage the spiritual world; you can't control it with power.

The masculine side suffers from this. But understanding this gives us life forces.

Further, we need to cultivate the quality of joy. What a wonderful thing, that we are allowed to be here on earth! Sadly, we are often too shy to show it outwardly. Children look at the adults around them and see that we are stressed, overwhelmed, and joyless. But what they need is ecstasy! Joy is what we must give to our children. We must show them that we are grateful to be here, that this is a beautiful time to be here, because we are free to change so much on earth. When we are separated and uprooted from life itself, living in virtual reality, this leads youngsters to drugs, for they crave connection. Joy in being here makes us healthy and builds a connection to the physical body.

Love of every being and well-intended interest foster the quality of wonder. Well-intended interest and an understanding of life processes cultivate the quality of compassion. The understanding of life and the joy of being here on Earth stimulate the quality of conscience. The moral, conscious attitude that the qualities of wonder, compassion, and conscience bring about is what the world needs at this time.

How can we understand the role of evil in our times in the development of the child and of humanity?

There was a young man who was having difficulties with drugs in high school. While the school's college of teachers was meeting behind closed doors to discuss his case, the boy himself came into the room, shocking many. He said that whatever decision they made concerning his fate, he simply wanted to say, "You need me!" About half of the college, the ones who had him in class, concluded that this was the final insolence, while the other half thought that he might be speaking the truth. Ultimately he was given a leave of absence and then came back, and many issues that had been splitting the students, faculty, and parent body were resolved, for working out among themselves how best to engage this boy had the effect of building bridges among people.

This boy presented himself as an individuality in the process of becoming. He knew he was not problem-free, but he felt that because the adults around him were often overwhelmed and exhausted with their own lives, they didn't take the time or have the energy to cope with him. He called himself a "homeless individuality" who hadn't been able to find real friends. He also expressed frustration with the rapid pace and time pressures of life. He had a sense of being uprooted and disconnected. Finally, he accused the adults of not showing their joy in life.

This boy's experiences point to the many ways in which we have put our children's development at risk. We often do not give our children the chance to have a physical body that is penetrated and integrated with the etheric, or life body, and the astral body of wishes and desires. The physical body itself is under-developed due to poor nutrition, too many vaccinations, and insufficient development of the lower senses of movement, balance, touch, and life (or well-being). The modern result of this lack of proper unfolding and development in the lower senses is called ADD or ADHD.

Processes of development require time, and modern culture robs children of this time by demanding them to be little adults by age seven or eight or younger. We ask them to imitate adults far too early and do not allow them to be children anymore. As a result, we human beings feel exhausted, we feel lonely in community, and we feel dissociated from the stream of time. Rather, we feel driven or overwhelmed. We are unable to have a real encounter, because true meeting requires time and physical well-being. There are also fewer contexts for social encounter than there used to be. The impetus to meet must come from us. Freedom is the positive side of this new social reality, but the shadow side is loneliness. In the past, we found our security socially, in large groups. But the social group grows smaller and smaller. For example, now there are fewer extended family living situations and many more single parent households.

Ultimately, the ego faces its individual identity crisis. Going through the eye of the needle is the uncomfortable, but spiritually necessary choice each individuality faces. But it remains a choice, and some individualities retreat from that juncture. They do not want to go through, but turn back and align their egos with old associations of blood relationships, ethnicities, or nationalities. Alternatively they may numb themselves with TV, alcohol, drugs, addiction to criticism, and so forth. There are many ways to avoid going through. Each individual's decision to go through this narrow eye and reach the spirit self—or not—has consequences. It will make a difference to what can come in the future. And it is a decision that rests entirely in the inner realm of freedom belonging to each person.

Transforming Evil in Our Time

The tasks of realizing the consciousness soul and creating new forms of Michael-inspired, courageous, and creative community are upon us. This means that we must hold the balance and be able to live and cope in a world of contradictions. In Greek times, one side was good and the other evil, and one could discard the evil. Our task now is to see how the evil can serve the good. Both are necessary to our development. The evil might even be our own sleepy inertia, which keeps us from doing something out of our own inner activity. Even so, what hinders us now from going through the eye of the needle, and engaging our I, may prove to be a valuable detour containing necessary lessons. So a failure is no cause for judgment, nor is it the end of the story.

In the fifth lecture in *From Symptom to Reality*, Rudolf Steiner encourages us to perceive events of birth and death externally and to gain an understanding of repeated lives on earth. He mentions that in the fifth cultural epoch, evil is destined to develop in man's inner being, and he suggests that if we want to inquire into evil in the human being, we must look not only to society, but to tendencies inside the human being. We have to come to an important time of observing and acknowledging the role of evil in our time. How are evil tendencies active in mankind? We receive insight and answers to such questions when we try to gain a real understanding of the human being, since in this epoch evil tendencies are present in us all. Whether these tendencies lead to evil actions depends on other circumstances.

Picture a train traveling on the tracks. One might say that the function of a railway engine is to wear down the rails, for that is in fact what happens. However, the truth of it is that the wear is only a side effect, not the true intention. In the same way evil in our time does not exist for its own sake, but rather it awakens in mankind the life of the spirit by calling upon us to develop the consciousness soul.

Self-recognition is usually a painful process, born not out of harmonious and comfortable situations in life, but rather out of the contradictory and complex situations we face. This may give us an appreciation for the complicated social problems in our time even though we prefer harmony, joy, and happiness. Many Waldorf schools would like to have a director and save the time and energy used by arriving at decisions by consensus. But we have to go through social conflicts in order to be freer. Is it a wonder that our youngsters have trouble living with contradictions and balancing contradictory roles? They numb themselves with drugs, still imitating adults who numb themselves differently. If we blame our youngsters for not being able to cope with the fast pace of life and the difficult role of evil, we must realize that we are just as incapable.

To get at the roots of the phenomenon, we have to start with self-recognition. "Man recognize yourself," is the task of the fifth post-Atlantean cultural epoch. Ita Wegman, in *Out of the Working of Michael*, gave beautiful pictures of our Time Spirit, the Archangel Michael. Usually in these pictures a battle is represented in which a lower aspect is conquered by a higher one. The lower aspect involves a dragon, but there is also a being which voluntarily sacrifices itself and voluntarily accompanies the path of evil without being evil itself. That being is the preparer of the path, the angel whom Christ sent before Him and who is later called Elijah. The archangel who overshadows this angel is Michael.

The Archangel Michael holds sway wherever personalities are striving to develop. If we make judgments, saying that these developing personalities are evil, they become fixed in those perceptions and do become evil. What we need is the empathy to accompany these beings, to help them come through. An appropriate prayer might be: "Stop me from thinking in a fixed way about people who are caught up in criminal behavior, drug use, and so on. Help me to give them space." If I try to make the world good by stopping what I perceive as evil, then I stop development. And that is evil.

Victor Frankl was an Austrian therapist who died three years ago. In his work with prisoners he recognized his task as that of helping them to overcome the deeds they had done and the associated guilt while not judging them. His message was that they were human beings with a higher self. One prisoner observed that Frankl's work was successful because ". . . he looked at us as if our self-development was worthwhile."

So the main intention of evil is to awaken mankind for the spiritual self. The apparent negativity is like the worn railway tracks, a side effect or symptom. To recognize evil is to face it, not to exclude evil from the developmental path. At the critical moment we must ask ourselves, "Am I a true companion to those young people who are entering a path of evil?" If we accompany them to that abyss, they may make it.

A further aspect of being non-judgmental was illumined by another boy who was sent to my office by the school authorities for drug issues. The boy entered my office clearly uncomfortable, not free, and started by saying he wasn't sure exactly why he was there. I simply reflected his statements back to him until he started to come forth with the situation. The boy said, "The teachers say that I have problems with my will because I use hashish. I was told you could make it go away." I responded, "I'm not willing to be your next drug." I continued to reflect his statements back to him for most of the hour, and I finally said, "I can't stop your hash consumption for you." Six weeks later he called to tell me he had quit, although I had never told him to quit. He himself had decided to do it. Young people need space. It is okay to have a moral point of view, but it is not for judgment. When we judge people, we make them passive.

Evil is a force that can destroy mankind or develop mankind, and the outcome depends on the quality of the social encounter. In *From Symptom to Reality*, Rudolf Steiner talks about facing evil in a positive way. He says there have to be new qualities of encounter on a higher level.

Supporting healthy child development in the challenging sensory environment of our times:

A medical study of six-year-olds entering schools in Germany shows the tendencies of our times. Of those children entering school: 34% have allergies, 20% come to school without breakfast, 30% have "backbone" (spinal, structural) problems, 60% have sleeping disorders, 37% are overweight (wrongly nourished), 61% live in a smoking addicted environment, and 15% live in abusive surroundings. Facing this, we can no longer say: "Childhood isn't that bad," or "These are neglected groups that do not belong to the mainstream of society." This is part of life. It hurts to experience these children who suffer.

Many of the youngsters in our schools, perhaps with some of these symptoms, fear becoming adults. They don't feel sheltered in this world, or secure in their physical body. In Germany, forty-five children a day try to commit suicide. Victor Frankl found that in the United States half a million young people a year are trying to kill themselves just before college. These children look back to a childhood in which they tried to withdraw (through anorexia, for example), or isolate themselves (through technological, computerized pursuits), so that they would not need to communicate with the world anymore.

Children and adolescents are suffering from depression and from its counterpart, aggression. Against this background, young people long more than ever to have time and to be left in peace by adults and teachers. They long for sanctuaries.

How can we support healthy child development in the challenging sensory environment of our time? This is not easy. There is no simple recipe. First we must ask, "What is a healthy childhood? What qualities stand behind a healthy childhood?"

When a child is first born, there is a certain holy atmosphere around him or her. The spiritual realm around the child touches us deeply. We can try to find words to describe the vestiges of this quality that can remain in kindergarten.

- **Trust:** What is so touching is that no matter what surroundings a child is born into, all children have trust. No matter what kind of house they are born into, they want to adore somebody. But do they find enough people worthy of adoration?

- **Play:** Children are absolutely invested in everything they do. They cannot split themselves and do two things at once— only adults can do this. Children lose themselves in play and forget time and space. They create a world of fantasy in which anything can become anything. This is the danger inherent in fixed toys. They do not allow the child's fantasy to transform them into anything else.

- **No masks:** Children are what they are; they live without masks. And, if they take on a role, they tell us beforehand: "I am a princess now." They are completely identified with themselves.

- **Forgiveness:** An essential quality of childhood is that children can forgive anything, even abuse. This is a very deep, unconscious quality of the child.

We are living in a society of unforgiveness, mistrust, disrespect, and multi-tasking. Childhood forces seem to be the opposite of adult society. The task of the Waldorf teacher is to make sure children have and keep these qualities, to cultivate an inner knowledge of these qualities and act so as not to jeopardize them.

The Environment of Children Today

What characterizes the environment of children today?

- **Products:** In society there is the general attitude of: "If you've got it, flaunt it." The idea is that the possession of products makes one's identity. The consciousness of brands is strong even in kindergarten.

- **Media:** We suffer greatly from passivity caused by media and electronic toys. Sense passivity is killing the life processes that want to be developed. Passivity through media is a very serious pathology in our time.

- **Loss of power:** We are losing our power to grapple with these realities. We give up the fight. Over the TV issue, for example, we should not ask parents to make contracts such as: "Your child is allowed to enter this Waldorf school if you promise that your child won't watch television until the age of ten." Perhaps some parents can accomplish this, but many cannot. But they sign up, and a schizophrenic pattern of untruth is created.

- **Loss of speech and language:** We are losing our capacity for speech and language. Research shows that children's language skills do not improve beyond a third grade level if they watch television for three hours a day from the age of four. Our ability to communicate with others through words is being stunted. Barry Sanders, author of *A is for Ox: The Collapse of Literacy and the Rise of Violence in an Electronic Age*, writes: "Pistols are the writing instruments of the illiterates." When children are not able to communicate their emotions with words, then feelings and aggressiveness are thrust to a lower level.

- **Schools support economy:** Schools are starting to be places for the selection of a professional career, institutions that support economic growth and professional career choices. They are ceasing to be places for the building up of human capacities and social skills.

- **Short lessons:** Building up a new process of will in the rhythm of forty-five-minute lessons does not work. This time limit stops the lesson before the process enters the child's will. The time must be lengthened. There must be a minimum of one hour per lesson in addition to the two-and-a-half hour main lesson block in the morning.
- **Utilitarian environment:** School environments are more and more functional, devoid of fantasy. Some of the German government kindergarten buildings are equipped with computers. Four- and five-year-old children enter these rooms every morning.

In summary: We are living in a crisis! To give up qualities of childhood is to give up on the future. The future lies in the forces of childhood. We adults are also yearning to get back these forces on a conscious level: to be able to forgive, to be social, to adore something beyond ourselves, to dedicate ourselves to a goal or task. We yearn for this. If we don't give our children the possibility of having these childhood qualities, then in their children these qualities will never arise.

Crisis is positive. The word comes from the Greek and means "decision." Mankind is at the point of decision. We have to decide about our society. Each of us must be a fighter for the qualities of childhood. Another issue we have to struggle with, even in the kindergarten, is aggression and violence. What is the deeper source of aggressiveness and violence, of senseless, unanticipated, violence? When do we ourselves become aggressive?

At one time in my life I suffered with shoulder and neck trauma and was stressed by pain. The anthroposophical doctor advised me to have a MRI to find the reason for the problem. I had no knowledge of MRI, but I went to the MRI room, disrobed, and got on the table. The assistant left the room and spoke over the loudspeaker, "We are driving now." I disappeared into an apparently unending tunnel. As I lay in the tunnel, a voice said, "If you need to breathe, breathe shallowly." Then there was a huge clanking noise. Depressed, I thought that the tunnel was broken, so I pushed the alarm button and got out. The assistant came with a syringe of Valium, but I said, "I don't need Valium. I need to understand how this works." I was taken around, shown how the mechanism worked, and was then able to survive inside the tunnel for half an hour without the sedation.

This must be the inner feeling of our children, whose real needs for development are not considered in an appropriate way. They must feel stuck, in a tunnel-like physical body that is not flexible enough. Children are not being well served by their environment, and this is a source of aggressiveness. If we are hungry or have had too little sleep, we start to be aggressive. When sixty percent of children have sleeping disorders, it is healthy to become aggressive! It is a shout for help: There is something wrong being done with me! We must become researchers into the problem, not with blame, but with a loving interest in the child. But in order to engage in this research, we need to have time for our children, time which is so often not given to them.

There is a wonderful book in German, which tells the true story of an eleven-year-old Norwegian boy named Morton, who was sick with terminal cancer. He read a column for children somewhere and wrote a letter in response. His letter caused an avalanche of letters from children all over Norway. The journalist who was receiving all these letters, a seventy-year-old man, went to help Morton work with the letters, to try to answer them. These two became friends. Then Morton said: "We will write a book, and I will say which letters will appear in it." Toward the end, Morton didn't want to hear any letters from adults, only from children under ten.

Morton wrote, in a letter to his parents, "If I had written before my illness, I would have said I have had a bad life. Mama and Papa were so busy. I am an only child. I got lots of presents, which my friends didn't, but it would have been better to be home with my parents, with time. When my parents realized I was sick, suddenly they had time. They say often, now, how much they love me. They never said this before—and I wouldn't have believed it. Dear Mother, now you are pregnant again. Do me a favor. Don't make the same mistake again."

The main task of education in our time is to bring the deepest activity into childhood. What does this mean? We must give children the chance to develop their lower senses fully, especially the sense of touch. We must give children space for physical movement. If there is not space at home or on the street, then parents have to take their children outside into nature at least three or four times a week.

Why does Huckleberry Finn never get addicted? Huckleberry Finn has a drunken father, no mother, is neglected, has no Waldorf kindergarten, and no music lessons. But he does have nature. He lives almost entirely in nature. He swings on the trees, jumps in the water. He does everything with his lower senses that he can do. He gets muddy and dirty. There is no father or mother taking him away from these activities because they could be too dangerous. And later in life, he is able to cope with situations that are not joyful, because he had so much joy before!

Let us give our children an active time of joy. Then they can face conflict. To let the sense of touch be developed helps the child build trust in the higher world, trust in other ego-beings. Whenever children have only one material (such as all plastic toys) there is no differentiation. The sense of touch becomes limited. You have a different feeling touching nylon or silk. Give children many sense experiences. Say "yes" to the physical body! This gives the children a foundation for all that comes next.

Felicitas Vogt is a former Waldorf school class teacher who has taken a deep interest in the problems of students drawn to drug use. She travels throughout the world inspiring parents and teachers to develop a deeper understanding of children and youth and to find new depths of compassion in serving them. She is also the former director of the Verein für Anthroposophisches Heilwesen, an anthroposophical organization for patients' rights. She is currently working as a lecturer, a cabaret actor and author. This article was written from notes from Felicitas Vogt's lectures at the East Coast Kindergarten Conference in February 2000 by Kate Gage and Sandi Chamberlin of Acorn Hill Waldorf Kindergarten in Silver Spring, Maryland.

The Path of Inner Schooling

Jorgen Smit

Self-education is more than the acquisition of knowledge. We arrive at a point where we feel it makes no sense to stay at the same plane of consciousness any longer. This is a point of awakening. No one can require this of another. This must be a free decision on each person's part. Then the path of esoteric schooling can begin. If we ask, what can small children do, we could easily answer "nothing." They cannot yet speak a foreign language, do arithmetic problems, et cetera. In comparison, adults can do a great deal. But if we consider the human soul in relationship to knowledge of higher worlds, then adults can do nothing. They have not yet begun. One aspect of self-education is intellectual humility, the ability to say, "I am at the beginning. I have not yet begun this inner esoteric schooling."

But intellectual humility alone does not suffice for our journey of inner schooling. We also need intellectual courage. We need to be able to say, "I must go on this path into the future." Either aspect alone does not work. Both are needed, and together they make a whole that allows doors to open along the path of inner development.

Consider the exercise from *How to Know Higher Worlds* which requires that one contemplate that which is budding and growing in contrast to that which is fading and dying. In spring it is easy to see both – the new buds opening and last summer's leaves which are brown and fading. These phenomena give rise to different feelings in us. We cannot "produce" the feeling. The soul itself must answer our intense observation, and the feelings resulting from observation become stronger and more differentiated. Note exactly how Rudolf Steiner describes the resulting sensation in the description of the exercise. He offers pictures that can be living examples, yet he is very exact in his descriptions. Through such exercises the inner qualities of feeling will grow and develop, and a new world will emerge.

Another exercise is the concentration exercise for control of thinking. Spend five minutes thinking about some small man-made object. This takes us in the opposite direction of the above exercise and helps develop will in our thinking. The balance of these two approaches is needed—developing the soul forces alone could lead to selfishness and egotism.

It is important to work on ourselves as well, to bring the light of consciousness into the dark realm of our will forces. Look on yourself from the "outside." Begin with small things such as habitual gestures such as crossing arms and legs. Discover the small things that you do without knowing that you do them. When we decide not to do this gesture, but to do another in its place, we find it is more difficult to change than we might have thought. There are strong forces within us which resist change, but it is possible to change, beginning with small things. It is too much to say, "From now on I will be a good person," but one can bring out change when one starts with small things.

We can also review our own biography, looking at ourselves as if we were a stranger. We can select a dramatic situation and look back at ourselves at a younger age and try to se what was essential and what was not essential. This can be accomplished by looking from a higher point of view. Separate the surface details from the inner forces of development that were the essential factors in the life situation. Then we can begin to ask, "Who was with me?" In this way we get beyond ourselves and begin to perceive others who were essential, and who were working into our own life. We are "diving into the other" and going beyond ourselves.

There are two aspects to inner work. One is the development of an inner life; the other is bringing consciousness into the will forces. The more intensive one aspect is, the further the other can go. It is like breathing, an alternation between self–knowledge and world knowledge.

On this path of inner schooling there are three important stages. These three occur in every event of life, whether great or small.

1. Strengthening your own inner forces, allowing them to grow outwards.
2. Opening yourself like a chalice or bowl so that the spiritual world may come in and speak to you. Be inwardly silent.
3. Uniting yourself within the spiritual world that has begun to speak in you. (You cannot do this at first.) This is then a deeply religious experience.

In daily exercises, where we build on what we did yesterday, we must take into account what happened during sleep. If this sleep experience were not there, we could not do anything during the day. We would die. During sleep–life all the forces of renewal, of ripening, come into our life. They are just as important as our day-life. The two go together. Real self-development alternates between sleeping and waking and unites them. Night and day weave back and forth around the line of self-development like the caduceus figure. This is the Mercury symbol of healing and was discussed in Dr. Kranich's lecture. At first we are only aware of the daytime consciousness. When we place it in its right context, it goes into a deeper and higher realm. Then we find a higher part of ourselves and we change.

How can we help the small child? Can we help him if we do not find in ourselves these true forces of self-development? We can help the small child if we are following this path of inner schooling, if we bring together day and night consciousness for individual development. Forces also come from the child to help the teacher. There is a meeting between the two. The young child is still close to the spiritual world. He brings this world to the teacher. In the second seven years, the children can still offer the teachers something, but the children have now "fallen." In the third seven years, after puberty, the students have the least spiritual forces to offer. That is why they are the hardest to work with. Yet our task is most difficult in working with small children in one sense, because we must work with the highest spiritual forces.

We must not neglect our work with the parents as well. Children are in the kindergarten only a few hours each day, so it is especially vital that we educate the parents. In our spiritual work it is important that we do not hold empty concepts. Rudolf Steiner told the story about himself as a child throwing plates on the floor after he had eaten the food and they were empty. His mother had to watch carefully to protect her dishes. Yet it was this same trait, transformed into an adult form, that appeared later in his work as a spiritual scientist when he wished to throw away empty concepts and share living thoughts. Once Steiner said it would be good if each week we could formulate our spiritual thoughts in a new way so that they did not become empty vehicles. Formulated schemes are like empty plates—if they are not filled with living food then they, too, should be thrown away.

Jorgen Smit was a Waldorf teacher from Norway who became the leader of the Pedagogical Section at the Goetheanum in Dornach. He lectured throughout the world on the inner aspects of Waldorf education.

Spiritual Foundations of Waldorf Education

Michaela Glöckler, M.D.

Our times are characterized by a tremendous contradiction or discrepancy, which we can all feel, between two realities. One is the feeling of impotence in the face of outer circumstances and threats, such as terrible wars and the pollution of nature. The other is the possibility for individual freedom and responsibility for our own destiny. The times are no longer as they were when one person, such as Charlemagne, could rule large sections of the world. Today we have more freedom, including the possibility for individual thinking and for ruling ourselves.

As an indication of this new freedom in thought, every child today learns to read and write, which was never formerly the case. We each want to think individually, and we each feel a responsibility for our own destiny. Yet this individualism can go too far if we do not also have the idea that we share a common future as humanity. If our sense of autonomy grows too great, then each will pull against the other, and we will experience what Rudolf Steiner called the "all against all." It is necessary to develop a sense of community, seeing humanity as an organism, each one a part of the whole. We have a common future. This is the Christ impulse. This is a basic aspect of Waldorf education: respect for the development of the individual while at the same time cultivating a sense of responsibility for the whole. Developing a sense of responsibility requires reincarnation. We need to experience what we have done wrong. If we stand by and allow nuclear plants to be built and do not return in one thousand years to accept responsibility for these actions, we will not grow. We need reincarnation to gain responsibility.

What do we mean by the word "freedom?" It is a space in which one can grown and grow. In this space is the sum of all our abilities with which we can work. Freedom recognizes certain limitations. For example, we must study certain things to become an engineer. The freedom to act as an engineer comes after accepting the requirements and limitations of study and preparation. Thus in our life, freedom is reached by working through the suffering and situations that meet us. We must reach the ability to offer our gifts, to decide in which direction we will work. Many incarnations are needed to develop more qualities and abilities and thus to experience greater freedom. This is linked with our destiny and karma, which is an individual matter and cannot be shared. Yet at the same time, we as individuals are bound together through the Christian idea of the social future of mankind.

To find a personal connection with the reality of the Christ is most important for us in working with children and in going toward the future. We cannot get this from hearing about it. We must experience it ourselves. It is not true when people say, "You need to be clairvoyant to experience the Christ or to know the spiritual world." Clairvoyance is not necessary to be convinced of the Mystery of Golgotha. You must be able to think and then feel whether your thoughts are true. Thoughts are a spiritual reality. In connection with this, Rudolf Steiner cites mathematical studies as training for spiritual development, for it helps develop pure thought, sense-free and exact. We must live and experience our own thoughts. We must find our own convictions about the Christ. This is not something we can learn from others, not even from the Gospel! This is something that we must experience.

When we look at Rudolf Steiner's statue of the Group, we look at the central figure, the *Representative of Man,* and we have this feeling: Here is a being whose facial expression shows concentration and clarity. He is filled with light, with clear *thoughts.* If he opened his mouth, he would speak the truth. He cannot lie. I have faith in that which he would say. We look at his gesture and see that he is not standing still, but is in a position of striding. He fights against evil, and his arms are his swords. He is not aggressive, but has a calm, strong and sure gesture with which he holds evil in its place.

This being has three weapons in his struggle against evil:

Clear thought—Thinking

Ability to speak the truth—Speaking

Forward movement—Walking

Today many people no longer know how to move forward. There is a paralysis in the will forces, and many people cannot inwardly move. They have a sense of a "dead end."

Yet at the same time it is possible to catch glimpses of something higher. We are engaged in a constant search for balance, rather than informing judgments that this is right or this is wrong. We must build on small things—humility, not egotism —the will to move ahead. With a goal we can move towards the future and not be overwhelmed by a sense that life is unbearable.

We can look at the young child and see the similarities with the figure of the Representative of Man. The child has the same powers as those depicted in the statue. The two-year-old cannot lie. It is impossible. Only when self-knowledge enters can lying begin, only when we learn to hide ourselves as Adam and Eve did before God.

We come to the question of why Waldorf education is so important. The first lighting up of the ego, the I, comes in the third year while the child still needs much protection. The body is only slowly becoming an instrument for the I. The child is still carrying the gifts of the spiritual world, but he is being awakened intellectually at a very early age. There comes then a discrepancy for the child who cannot reconcile these things. Waldorf education must harmonize this discrepancy. For the young child, the will is developed through imitation. In the grades, the child is oriented through loving authority, but it is an objective love that goes beyond sympathy or antipathy. After adolescence, there is an emergence of clear thinking and intellectual growth.

The goal of Waldorf education is to help the consciousness of the self to develop slowly until the physical and soul organism is fully mature. Then the individual can act in freedom. If the necessity of acting comes too early, the discrepancy between willing and feeling will remain too great. There is also the question of how we can help the parents.

Listen to their questions, and see where they are. Don't come at them dogmatically, but rather awaken development in them. The younger the child comes to us, the more possibility there is of reaching the parents.

When we look at the small child learning to walk, to speak and to think we can experience three "wonders" in the child's development. First, the child is never angry that he has to learn so much. He is not angry that in one year he must learn to walk. Secondly, in learning to speak the child cannot lie. And thirdly, when the child is learning to think, he experiences a love of learning. Around the age of three, when the child begins to say I, he is using these qualities of walking, speaking and thinking. They are necessary for him if he is to say, "I."

As beautiful as this process of saying, "I" is, it can also come too early in the life of the child. There is a discrepancy between what the soul desires and what the individual can do. We must protect the unfolding self-consciousness of the child until the body is ready to be a vessel for the I. That is why Waldorf education must protect the child. In the early years this protection takes place through imitation. In the grades it takes place through authority, and in adolescence intellectual thought develops after puberty at the end of the bodily ripening. Then the Waldorf student develops his self-consciousness and says, "I go where I will." Now the young person is ready to say I, but if this comes too soon, he will have difficulty coming to the true living Christ. If his organs of perception are closed, he will not be able to achieve the higher possibilities described in *How to Know Higher Worlds*.

The teacher must develop gestures that appear human, for example as in eurythmy. He or she must work out of an awareness of speech, and must educate thinking in such a way that it has clarity. Then the qualities of early childhood will be re-awakened in us. We will again have learned to walk, to speak and to think. Then we can develop an organ of perception for experiencing the Christ.

Every child shows us how to develop these qualities. Then later in our life we can truly say, "I," we can see how much too soon the first I is and how great the need is for protection if the recognition of the true I is to come. In the cycle of the year, each festival has its own particular soul quality. At Easter, we experience the love that accompanies man's development. The resurrection forces are within us, and the face of helplessness there is a new strength that comes. Michaelmas has a different quality. Michael is there to be called on. He will not intervene; we must call on him and unite with him if we are to go forward. Then we come to know that the more possibilities we have to work in the world, the greater is our freedom, the greater our possibilities, the more we can do.

Dr. Michaela Glöckler is currently the head of the Medical Section of the School of Spiritual Science in Dornach, Switzerland. She has been active as a pediatrician and school doctor in Germany and is the author of A Guide to Child Health, *Floris Books.*

www.ingramcontent.com/pod-product-compliance
Lightning Source LLC
Chambersburg PA
CBHW080549170426
43195CB00016B/2731